15 Chicago Poets

15 Chicago Poets

Edited by:
Richard Friedman
Peter Kostakis
Darlene Pearlstein

cop. a

Milk Quarterly 9 & 10

The Yellow Press—Chicago—1976

ACKNOWLEDGEMENTS: Some of these poems have appeared in the following periodicals: *Brilliant Corners*, Broadside Press *Broadside #31*, *Chicago*, *Here It Is*, *Mati*, *Oink!*, *Out There*, *The Paris Review*, *Poetry Now* and *Stone Wind*. Thanks are due to their editors.

Additional acknowledgement of prior publication in book form to: poems from *A Feeling for Leaving* copyright © 1975 by Ted Berrigan, Frontward Books; "The Life of Lincoln West" © 1970 by Gwendolyn Brooks from *Family Pictures*, reprinted with permission from Broadside Press; "Riot" © 1969 by Gwendolyn Brooks from *Riot*, reprinted with permission from Broadside Press; "Horses Graze" © 1975 by Gwendolyn Brooks from *Beckonings*, reprinted with permission from Broadside Press; "Resignation Day" © 1975 by Richard Friedman from *Straight*, The Yellow Press; "We Walk the Way of the New World" © 1971 by Haki R. Madhubuti (Don L. Lee) from *We Walk the Way of the New World*, reprinted with permission from Broadside Press; and "Positive Movement Will Be Difficult but Necessary" © 1973 by Haki R. Madhubuti (Don L. Lee) from *Book of Life*, reprinted with permission from Broadside Press.

ISBN 0-916328-03-1 (paperback)
ISBN 0-916328-04-X (cloth)

Thanks to CCLM and The Illinois Arts Council.

Yellow Press books are distributed by
Serendipity Books
1790 Shattuck Avenue
Berkeley, California 94709
Address all orders to them.

The Yellow Press
2394 Blue Island Avenue
Chicago, Illinois 60608

Cover Photo and Design by Mike Tappin

to our parents

CONTENTS

15 Chicago Poets

Gerard Malanga

TED BERRIGAN

Ted Berrigan was born in 1934 in Providence, Rhode Island. He received a B.A. and an M.A. from Tulsa University. Was the editor of "C" magazine and "C" books in New York City in the sixties. Author of *Bean Spasms* (with Ron Padgett and Joe Brainard from Kulchur Foundation), *The Sonnets* (Grove Press), *Many Happy Returns* (Corinth), *In The Early Morning Rain* (Cape Goliard Grossman), *Back in Boston Again* (with Tom Clark and Ron Padgett from Telegraph Books), and *A Feeling for Leaving* (Frontward Books). The Yellow Press will soon publish his next book of poems *Red Wagon*. Anthologized in *The Norton Anthology of Modern Poetry, The Young American Poets, An Anthology of New York Poets, Another World* and elsewhere. He has taught at The Iowa Writers Workshop, The University of Michigan, The University of Essex in England, and from January 1972 to January 1976 served as poet in residence at Northeastern Illinois University.

OLD-FASHIONED AIR

to Lee Crabtree

I'm living in Battersea, July,
1973, not sleeping, reading
Jet noise throbs building fading
Into baby talking, no, "speechifying"
"Ah wob chuk sh'guh!" Glee.
There's a famous Power Station I can't see
Up the street. Across there is
Battersea Park
I walked across this morning toward
A truly gorgeous radiant flush;
Sun; fumes of the Battersea
Power Station; London Air;
I walked down long avenues with trees
That leant not ungracefully
Over the concrete walk. Wet green lawn
Opened spaciously
Out on either side of me. I saw
A great flock of geese taking their morning walk
Unhurriedly.
I didn't hurry either, Lee.
I stopped & watched them walk back up toward
& down into their lake,
Smoked a Senior Service on a bench
As they swam past me in a long dumb graceful cluttered line,
Then, taking my time, I found my way
Out of that park;
A Gate that was locked. I jumped the fence.
From there I picked up the *London Times*, came home,
Anselm awake in his bed, Alice
Sleeping in mine: I changed
A diaper, read a small poem I'd had
In mind, then thought to write this line:
"Now is Monday morning so, that's a garbage truck I hear,
         not bells". . .
And we are back where we started from, Lee, you
         & me, alive & well!"

PICNIC

The dancer grins at the ground.
The mildest of alchemists will save him.
(Note random hill of chairs). & he will prove
      useful to her in time,
the ground to be their floor.

     like pennies to a three year old,
     like a novel, the right novel, to a 12 year old,
     like a 39 Ford to a Highschool kid
     like a woman is to a man, a girl
         who is a woman
             is her self's own soul
                and her man is himself
                   his own
                     & whole.

ADDENDA

   & I can't buy
            with submission
   & tho I feel often
             & why not
battered,
    I can't be beaten.

But I have been eaten, 7 times

    by myself

& I go my way, by myself, I being

by myself only when useful, as, for example,

  you are to me now,

        to you.

NEWTOWN

Sunday morning: here we live jostling & tricky
blues, blacks, reds & yellow all are gray
in each window: the urbanites have muscles
in their butts & backs; shy, rough, compassionate
& good natured, "they have sex in their pockets"
To women in love with my flesh I speak.
All the Irish major statements & half the best
Low-slung stone. Upstairs is sleep. Downstairs
is heat. She seems exceedingly thin and transparent
Two suspicious characters in my head. They park & then
Start, the same way you get out of bed. The pansy is
Grouchy. The Ideal Family awaits distribution on
The Planet. Another sensation tugged at his heart
Which he could not yet identify,
half Rumanian deathbed diamond
Wildly singing in the mountains with cancer of the spine.

THE END

Despair farms a curse, slackness
In the sleep of animals, with mangled limbs
Dogs, frogs, game elephants, while
There's your new life, blasted with milk.
It's the last day of summer, it's the first
Day of fall: soot sits on Chicago like
A fat head's hat. The quick abounds. Turn
To the left, turn to the right. On Bear's Head
Two Malted Milk balls. "Through not taking himself
Quietly enough he strained his insides." He
Encourages criticism, but he never forgives it.
You who are the class in the sky, receive him
Into where you dwell. May he rest long and well.
God help him, he invented us, that is, a future
Open living beneath his spell. One goes not where
One came from. One sitting says, "I stand corrected."

SO GOING AROUND CITIES

to Doug & Jan Oliver

"I order you to operate. I was not made to suffer."
Probing for old wills, and friendships, for to free
to New York City, to be in History, New York City being
History at that time." "And I traded my nights
for Intensity; & I barter my right to Gold; & I'd traded
my eyes much earlier, when I was circa say seven years old
for ears to hear Who was speaking, & just exactly who
was being told. . . ." & I'm glad
            I hear your words so clearly
            & I would not have done it
                        differently
            & I'm amused at such simplicity, even so,
inside each & every door. And now I'm with you, instantly,
& I'll see you tomorrow night, and I see you constantly, hopefully
though one or the other of us is often, to the body-mind's own self
more or less out of sight! Taking walks down any street, High
Street, Main Street, walk past my doors! Newtown; Nymph Rd
            (on the Mesa); Waveland
Meeting House Lane, in old Southampton; or BelleVue Road
            in England, etcetera
Other roads; Manhattan; see them there where open or shut up
behind
            "I've traded sweet times for answers. . .
"They don't serve me anymore." They still serve me on the floor.
            Or,
as now, as floor. Now we look out the windows, go in &
            out the doors. The Door.
(That front door which was but & then at that time My door).
            I closed it
On the wooing of Helen. "And so we left schools for her." For
She is not one bit fiction; & she is easy to see;
            & she leaves me small room
For contradiction. And she is not alone; & she is not one bit
            lonely in the large high room, &
invention is just vanity, which is plain. She
is the heart's own body, the body's own mind in itself
            self-contained.
& she talks like you; & she has created truly not single-handedly

6

Our tragic thing, America. And though I would be I am not afraid
    of her, & you also not. You, yourself, I,
Me, myself, me. And no, we certainly have not pulled down
    our vanity: but
We wear it lightly here,
            here where I traded evenly,
                     & even gladly
health, for sanity; here
           where we live day-by-day
                  on the same spot.
My English friends, whom I love & miss, we talk to ourselves here,
    & we two
rarely fail to remember, although we write seldom, & so must seem
    gone forever.
In the stained sky over this morning the clouds seem about to burst.
    What is being remembering
Is how we are, together. Like you we are always bothered, except
    by the worst; & we are living
    as with you we also were
fired, only, mostly, by changes in the weather. For Oh dear hearts,
When precious baby blows her fuse / it's just our way
    of keeping amused.
That we offer of & as excuse. Here's to you. All the very best.
    What's your pleasure? Cheers.

THE JOKE & THE STARS

What we have here is Animal Magick: the fox
is crossing the water: he is the forest from whence
he came, and toward which he swims: he is the hawk
circling the waters in the sun; and he is the foxfire
on each bank in Summer wind. He is also the grandfather clock
that stands in the corner of the room, one eye open,
    both hands up.

And though I am an Irishman in my American

I have not found in me one single he or she
who would sit on a midden and dream stars; for
Although I hate it, I walk with the savage gods.

"It's because you are guilty about being another person,
isn't it?" But back at the organ
The angel was able to play a great green tree
for the opening of the new First National Bank.

And New York City is the most beautiful city in the world
And it is horrible in that sense of hell. But then
So are you: and you, and you, and you, and you, and you.
And no I don't mean any of you; I just mean you.

BOULDER

Up a hill, short
of breath , then breathing

up stairs, & down, & up, & down again

to

NOISE

Your warm powerful Helloes
friends,
still slightly breathless

in
a three-way street
hug

Outside

& we can move
& we move   Inside

to STARBURSTS   of Noise!

The human voice is how.

Lewis's, boyish & clear;   & Allen's, which persists,

& His,   & Hers,   & All of them them thems!

                              & then
Anne's, once again, (and as I am)   "Ted!"

             Then

O, Lady!,   O, See, among all things which exist

O this!, this breathing, we.

CHICAGO MORNING

Under a red face, black velvet shyness
Milking an emaciated gaffer. God lies down
Here. Rattling of a shot engine, heard
From the first row. The president of the United States
And the Director of the FBI stand over
A dead mule. "Yes, it is nice to hear the fountain
With the green trees around it, as well as
People who need me." Quote Lovers of speech unquote. It's
       a nice thought
& typical of a rat. And, it is far more elaborate
Than expected. And the thing is, we don't *need*
      that much money.
Sunday morning; blues, blacks, red & yellow wander
In the soup. Grey in the windows' frames. The angular
Explosion in the hips. A huge camel rests
      in a massive hand
Casts clouds a smoggish white out & up over the Loop, while
Two factories (bricks) & a fortress of an oven (kiln)
Rise, barely visible inside a grey metallic gust.
      "The Fop's Tunic."
She gets down, off of the table, breaking a few more plates.
Natives paint their insides crystal white here (rooms)
Outside is more bricks, off-white. Europe at Night.

WALTER BRADFORD

Walter Bradford was born in Chicago in 1937. Founding member and organizer of The Organization of Black American Culture. Organized and conducted workshops with The Black P. Stone Nation and other youth groups. Anthologized in *Jump Bad, To Gwen With Love* and *Heartlands II*. His poems have appeared in Nommo, Black World, Journal of Black Poetry, Black Expressions, and The Broadside Press. Editor of *Lyrics of Locked up Ladies* (Center of Inner City Studies, Northeastern Illinois University)—poems which evolved from workshops taught at Cook County Jail, Women's Division. Winner of 1969 Gwendolyn Brooks Traveling Writing Fellowship. Has taught at Roosevelt University and was an artist in residence at Malcolm X College. Director of The Production Company, "Changes" and active with The Illinois Arts Council Poets in the Schools Program.

CHICAGO CENTENNIAL OR: THE TOWN HALL MEETING

In the winter of 73-74, Phillip Michael Irving
[This may not be the correct spelling of his
name, that information is unavailable.]
was killed by a Chicago policeman in a coffee
shop on north Broadway. The police investigated.
It was ruled a justifiable homocide. The incident
occured in the Town Hall district. The shop is a
candy store now.

Phillip Michael Irving
died at twenty-four.
The murder was Chicago. Typical northside,
on a coffee shop floor
where you got what you ordered quick to go out, quick,
to go on your way.
Phillip didn't know and before he could
two supersilver bullets opened his body split
like a drum made mute flash, he was present
flash, he was gone, subtracted from the world
this 1950 predestrian caught bowgish
like a street arab in a dance he didn't arrange
and was sent or what remained was sent south
to Mecca or wherever disposed arabs go.
He could boogie, he could get down
in his swoop green coat trimmed
with du pont leatherette, a Smoky Joe's ancient,
jewtown special, plaid buffalo baggies, the suit
of soul city, his biddy bowler, cap balero,
made him assertive, authentic and thoroughly absolute.
In paladium platforms, the double stacked heels
he leaned oblique
like a great wounded star, danced adagio

a street strut before our eyes they snatched his soul
from its moorings, his heart tumbled out
in the dust, used gum and shoebottoms,
we stood in his blood.
The murderer's hand
was a whiteman's hand
that trembled like it was sorry or stunned or shocked
at what it had done
to crumple Phillip's body that way.
But what could he do
towards a black boy suicide
enough to snatch his roscoe.

NEW NEWS

from the BLUE STAR MURDER MACHINE

Youngman black shot dead

provoked by color madness

america sings.

Phillip worshipped an ethic
he never really understood;
all his dreams, all his drama,
all his catechism died in order,
killed by the gospel and facetious puritan hymns;
they wore his magic out,
crushed his acrylic soul. With deeds and words,
I pray improvements, somehow, here, in this chapter
of grim and severe mistakes; I reach out,
my hand to God, I receive
a stone.

83RD STREET CHICAGO, 1969
SCENE AT THE SALAAM RESTAURANT

Egypt flows there
with different Pharaohs now,
Roosevelt, Little Junior, Sonnyboy and 'nem
newly ordained L.C. Ali,
all in the manner of the Honorable One.
Richland, Egyptland swirled in plastic golden-glow
leaps from walls
where shadows take no space
but give light, strengthful light
all in the manner of the Honorable One.
And late Nubians we
come early like the morning
calling birds from the sky, spirits from the moon
to be filled with the light, strengthful light,
all in the manner of the Honorable One.

WHEN HIP WAS KING

When hip was king,
Malcolm was a popcorn pimp
with no reputation,
Candy couldn't count money
til he got his first hog,
Wicked Willie Janks fled warm Georgia
worked sidewalks and shortstreets
earned each move he made.

Enter Joe The Grinder, sweetspot finder,
money in he pocket a mile long
played everything; 'hoes to harmonicas,
flim-flammed his spare time away,
Michigan Bankroll he flash gordon
on chumps who swore hustlin' was a
git all the way down to it, hip
game played, they thought
they could win.

T.C.
(Terry Callier; True Christian)

And the voices dropped
                    from the ashy ceiling like pellets of rain
foreshadowing his coming;
                    "A Gemini's Sun" they cried, "born to trudge
between the parallels of the heavenly twins."
    And he does that with a guitar for a crucifix and six thin
palms for strings (all of them mean actors)
                    while strolling down the dan
ry-an eXpressway, with a forty pound VOO DOO radiator on his
    back and
a red ban-dan-na tied around his head singing, "I have seen all the
light!"
        While some stillborn monkey niggahs
                    with steel knuckles for asses
in chartreuse pants and fishtail shoes, swing ape-style on the 51st
street overpass screaming: "Moses, is you back again?"
    And they streamed on behind him till the concreteness
        stopped at
the base of MECCA'S hill
                    just to hear

TERRY CALLIER SING!
And young 63rd street pharaohs cloaked in Blackstone's label
gave
peace hosannas to Disciples, for
creation was order, it was peace.
So instead of some bible-fiction god rebuilding this world let
Nommo-child Terry Callier sing the first seven days.
True christian, please make your world.

Mike Tappin

GWENDOLYN BROOKS

Gwendolyn Brooks was born in Topeka, Kansas June 1917, but she grew up in Chicago with schooling at Englewood High and Wilson Junior College. Recipient of a Pulitzer Prize for her book *Anne Allen*, she has been accorded the honor of appointment as Poet Laureate of Illinois. Recent books include *Family Pictures*, *Report from Part One* (autobiography), *Beckonings* and a volume of selected poems.

RIOT

> A riot is the language of the unheard.
> —MARTIN LUTHER KING

John Cabot, out of Wilma, once a Wycliffe,
all whitebluerose below his golden hair,
wrapped richly in right linen and right wool,
almost forgot his Jaguar and Lake Bluff;
almost forgot Grandtully (which is The
Best Thing That Ever Happened To Scotch); almost
forgot the sculpture at the Richard Gray
and Distelheim; the kidney pie at Maxim's,
the Granadine de Boeuf at Maison Henri.

Because the Negroes were coming down the street.

Because the Poor were sweaty and unpretty
(not like Two Dainty Negroes in Winnetka)
and they were coming toward him in rough ranks.
In seas. In windsweep. They were black and loud.
And not detainable. And not discreet.

Gross. Gross. "*Que tu es grossier!*" John Cabot
itched instantly beneath the nourished white
that told his story of glory to the World.
"Don't let It touch me! the blackness! Lord!" he whispered
to any handy angel in the sky.

But, in a thrilling announcement, on It drove
and breathed on him: and touched him. In that breath
the fume of pig foot, chitterling and cheap chili,
malign, mocked John. And, in terrific touch, old
averted doubt jerked forward decently,
cried "Cabot! John! You are a desperate man,
and the desperate die expensively today."

John Cabot went down in the smoke and fire
and broken glass and blood, and he cried "Lord!
Forgive these nigguhs that know not what they do."

THE LIFE OF LINCOLN WEST

Ugliest little boy
that everyone ever saw.
That is what everyone said.

Even to his mother it was apparent—
when the blue-aproned nurse came into the
northeast end of the maternity ward
bearing his squeals and plump bottom
looped up in a scant receiving blanket,
bending, to pass the bundle carefully
into the waiting mother-hands—that this
was no cute little ugliness, no sly baby waywardness
that was going to inch away
as would baby fat, baby curl, and
baby spot-rash. The pendulous lip, the
branching ears, the eyes so wide and wild,
the vague unvibrant brown of the skin,
and, most disturbing, the great head.
These components of That Look bespoke
the sure fibre. The deep grain.

His father could not bear the sight of him.
His mother high-piled her pretty dyed hair and
put him among her hairpins and sweethearts,
dance slippers, torn paper roses.
He was not less than these,
he was not more.

As the little Lincoln grew,
uglily upward and out, he began
to understand that something was
wrong. His little ways of trying
to please his father, the bringing
of matches, the jumping aside at
warning sound of oh-so-large and
rushing stride, the smile that gave
and gave and gave—Unsuccessful!

Even Christmases and Easters were spoiled.

He would be sitting at the
family feasting table, really
delighting in the displays of mashed potatoes
and the rich golden
fat-crust of the ham or the festive
fowl, when he would look up and find
somebody feeling indignant about him.

What a pity what a pity. No love
for one so loving. The little Lincoln
loved Everybody. Ants. The changing
caterpillar. His much-missing mother.
His kindergarten teacher.

His kindergarten teacher—whose
concern for him was composed of one
part sympathy and two parts repulsion.
The others ran up with their little drawings.
He ran up with his.
She
tried to be as pleasant with him as
with others, but it was difficult.
For she was all pretty! all daintiness,
all tiny vanilla, with blue eyes and fluffy
sun-hair. One afternoon she
saw him in the hall looking bleak against
the wall. It was strange because the
bell had long since rung and no other
child was in sight. Pity flooded her.
She buttoned her gloves and suggested
cheerfully that she walk him home. She
started out bravely, holding him by the
hand. But she had not walked far before
she regretted it. The little monkey.

Must everyone look? And clutching her
hand like that. . . Literally pinching
it. . .

At seven, the little Lincoln loved
the brother and sister who
moved next door. Handsome. Well-

19

dressed. Charitable, often, to him. They
enjoyed him because he was
resourceful, made up
games, told stories. But when
their More Acceptable friends came they turned
their handsome backs on him. He
hated himself for his feeling
of well-being when with them despite—
Everything.

He spent much time looking at himself
in mirrors. What could be done?
But there was no
shrinking his head. There was no
binding his ears.

"Don't touch me!" cried the little
fairy-like being in the playground.

Her name was Nerissa. The many
children were playing tag, but when
he caught her, she recoiled, jerked free
and ran. It was like all the
rainbow that ever was, going off
forever, all, all the sparklings in
the sunset west.

One day, while he was yet seven,
a thing happened. In the down-town movies
with his mother a white
man in the seat beside him whispered
loudly to a companion, and pointed at
the little Linc.
"THERE! That's the kind I've been wanting
to show you! One of the best
examples of the specie. Not like
those diluted Negroes you see so much of on
the streets these days, but the
real thing.

Black, ugly, and odd. You
can see the savagery. The blunt

blankness. That is the real
thing."

His mother—her hair had never looked so
red around the dark brown
velvet of her face—jumped up,
shrieked "Go to—" She did not finish.
She yanked to his feet the little
Lincoln, who was sitting there
staring in fascination at his assessor. At the author of his
new idea.

All the way home he was happy. Of course,
he had not liked the word
"ugly."
But, after, should he not
be used to that by now? What had
struck him, among words and meanings
he could little understand, was the phrase
"the real thing."
He didn't know quite why,
but he liked that.
He liked that very much.

When he was hurt, too much
stared at—
too much
left alone—he
thought about that. He told himself
"After all, I'm
the real thing."

It comforted him.

HORSES GRAZE

Cows graze.
Horses graze.
They
eat
eat
eat.
Their graceful heads
are bowed
bowed
bowed
in majestic oblivion.
They are nobly oblivious
to your follies,
your inflation,
the knocks and nettles of administration.
They
eat
eat
eat.
And at the crest of their brute satisfaction,
with wonderful gentleness, in affirmation,
they lift their clean calm eyes and they lie down
and love the world.
The speak with their companions.
They do not wish that they were otherwhere.
Perhaps they know that creature feet may press
only a few earth inches at a time,
that earth is anywhere earth,
that an eye may see,
wherever it may be,
the Immediate arc, alone, of life, of love.
In Sweden,
China,
Afrika,
in India or Maine
the animals are sane;
they know and know and know
there's ground below
and sky
up high.

Mike Tappin

PAUL CARROLL

Paul Carroll was born 1927 in Chicago; to an Irish father who came from a farm near Toronto and made 8 million in South Side banking and real estate, and a mother who came from Austrian immigrants who worked in the factories and mills of South Chicago. Mt. Carmel High '45, University of Chicago, M.A. '52. Father of son named Luke. Professor of English and Acting Chairman of the Program for Writers, University of Illinois at Chicago Circle. Poetry editor, *Chicago Review*, 1957-59; editor and publisher, *Big Table*, 1959-61. Former President, The Poetry Center at the Museum of Contemporary Art. *Odes* (1968), *The Poem in Its Skin* (1968), *The Luke Poems* (1971); *The Satirical Letters of St. Jerome* (translation)(1956); editor: *The Edward Dahlberg Reader* (1965), *The Young American Poets* (1968).

WORDS FOR NERUDA

I

On hearing of your death over the radio in a Checker taxi

Where are you
now, deer-
heart? A wave in a photograph?
Or exploring the cities inside the seeds of certain melons?
Here comes Francis Jammes his face of leather the color of those
    yellow leaves carrying your books in birdcages of bamboo.
Your poems are parachutes.
You could be laughing with the ghosts of Inca poets around the
    big blue table in the inn shaped like a horse's hoof filled with
    the odor of the burning body of the god of clouds.
I love it when your poems turn into mirrors for the stones.
Wearing a mate's woolen watchcap you're standing on the deck
    of the ore boat inching like a caterpillar from the harbor
    of Chicago bound for the vast white pages of the Soo.
Death is a memory of rivers with no names.
Hydor son laloun en emoy. O Neruda. Father.
In spats and battered bowler he has begun the slow soft in-
    credibly elegant dance within the cube of sunlight in his cell
    in the Southern prison long ago: Mr. Bojangles. Last night
the rain was like many of your words: the burly octopus of our
    desires.
Today the rain that webs the Oak Street beach and Drake Hotel
    looks delicate as the stopwatch of an angel.
Everyday is the birthday of your books.

II

                    Leaves
                    amber now near November
as Burns' bones. Waves
stiffen across the concrete rocks on Oak Street beach. This camel
of a stone
in the hollow of my palm: like your
Elemental Odes; like the earth, alone; small
                    as a galaxy. Thank you for the pinecone.

III

When a man can remember when the rain was brother like
    another skin

he may be able to begin opening the doors inside of certain
    words

and meet Neruda in the room of waves where light is what the
    whales know in dreams of the time before there was water
    on this earth

UNIVERSITY OF ILLINOIS AT CHICAGO CIRCLE
                                LECTURE SERIES
THE DEPARTMENT OF SPANISH PRESENTS
                        PABLO NERUDA: A TRIBUTE
READINGS IN SPANISH AND ENGLISH AND
                            A FILM ON HIS LIFE
TUESDAY NOVEMBER 23 1971 2 PM
                        LECTURE CENTER D2

I

Riding to it feels like being in the bedroom in Rimini
    when Fellini's parents are conceiving him

II

The professors strive to liberate Neruda's words from their
    white exile on the page
Stone   A sister's tears   House of flowers   Elephant a telephone
    booth inside a jungle   Star   Pinecone
The words will find space inside of certain bodies here
And there stay the way a dream exists inside until it's time
    for an appearance on the screen of tongue
Permanent as a photograph of snow carpeting the Colorado
Or a jar of fireflies in a museum
Or the ghosts in telephones

ODE TO DELMORE SCHWARTZ

(For Hershel Reider, L'Shanau Tova Tikvausaynu)

"Remember: we are not natural beings, but supernatural beings."
Saul Bellow: *Humboldt's Gift*

Are you writing in a radiant place now, Delmore,
poems finer and even more naively mysterious than in your first
book, a miracle,
In Dreams Begin Responsibilities,
which would be going some, to say the least?
Would you leave a recent poem for me in case you've departed
to a deeper splendor
by the time I reach the one you're in (ass-
uming these hands that write these lines don't end up in the
other spot, there to dwell "In adamantine chains and penal
fire" for transgressions).
Put the poem upon a table I can know—the one, say, Blake
has written at, his fingers of white feathers or white waves,
that Mozartean, delicate teak table
in the 18th century drawingroom that appears, like Christ to
Cleophas and his friend, walking to the village of Emmaus,
suddenly a stranger to disciples who adored him, as *2001:
A Space Odyssey* concludes.
Or are you sitting in some White Horse Tavern in the sky,
Delmore, talking
with Dionysius Areopigatus about the celestials known as
Thrones and the nature of the lights in Plato's soul?
Or observing us, floating by in a UFO sailboat in the clouds

of carbon monoxide poison above Hackensack, New Jersey?—
clouds looking like the bloated octopus upon the beach as *La
Dolce Vita* ends, wallowing in that spiritual sewer which is
the despair of monks;
and are you juding our egregious indulgence as we step
on the gas
inside our Mack trucks taxis stationwagons Volks and Honda
hogs Mercedes-Benzs Fords and Chevy pickup vans and
campers, barrelling
down expressways snaking out of arteriosclerotic New York

City, strangling
the atmosphere you're sailing through, choking
the grass near fire hydrants decorated by the stars-and-stripes of
    Bicentennial, turning into toilets
the Passaic River and Atlantic Ocean as it immigrates to reach
    the beach at Coney Island,
infecting as if with syphilis, even the purest of the brothers of St
    Francis,
the fire in the hollow fennel-stalk.

All of the Presidents also are observing us.

It is Sunday night. The back porch of a house on Regal Road
    near Homewood, Illinois. Milk and oatmeal cookies on a
    table near the American Gothic radio. "Fireside chat time."
    The voice of FDR:
"My friends, I've been back among you for a decade as a
    healing pool here in Hot Springs, Arkansas, where
I watch and think about our country, and talk,
from time to time, with Honest Abe, who's been an oak these 50
    years in a prairie near Galena in northwestern Illinois,
who's been observing, too,
as has my cousin Teddy, a grizzly bear in Yellowstone looking at
    the cars,
LBJ's a rattlesnake in a forest preserve in Bucks County,
    Pennsylvania,
Jefferson's a Black for 60 years, running a general store in
    Wheeling, West Virginia,
General Washington's a dentist, in Maple City, in Vermont,
young Kennedy's a jock, coaching Chicanos in an inner-city
    highschool in Chicago.
Every other Friday night we gather in the Oval Room in the
    White House in the sky,
to discuss how citizens are handling the legacy of the land
    inherited by you.
Two nights ago we voted in this resolution which President
    Lincoln will describe to you."
"Good evening, my fellow Americans. This is what your Pres-
    idents decided: If
all Americans don't cease being accomplices in the rape of our
    environment future Americans shall have to share,
then tomorrow at 9 a.m. Central Standard Time,

all of your Presidents shall come again in flesh and bone upon
    the banks of the Potomac, wearing
khaki gasmasks from the War to End All Wars,
and each in turn will ask John F. Kennedy to read our message
    here to you:
'All American citizens must legislate laws forbidding the manu-
    facture and the use of anything and everything that
    assassinates the healing Hot Springs in Arkansas, all of the
    oaks in Illinois, the bears and snakes and babies in the bellies
    of Chicano-American mothers in the neighborhood around
    23rd and California in Chicago; or else,
all of the Presidents, as a body, shall declare:
As Commanders-in-Chief of the Armed Forces of the United
    States of America,
we hereby declare war on all that is polluting the air, earth,
    water and fire of America. The means of war we leave to
    your imaginations.'"

"This is Franklin Delano Roosevelt again. Your Presidents are
    confident, my friends, that our means of warfare will prove
    to be victorious; and that the worst enemy this country's had
    in its 200 years, shall soon disappear into the dark clouds at
    the center of the earth.   Then,
my fellow Americans, our great country shall no more have to
    hang its head in shame for our massive contribution to the
    pollution of the water of the buffalos in Bangladesh and the
    atmosphere around the planet Mars.
Good night, for now, my friends."

Your face in the double portrait in your *Selected Poems*,
    Delmore,
is like the sun cut-
ting splendiferous track of light on the lake
beyond my apartment on East Lake Terrace, in Chicago, here.
    Wait for me.

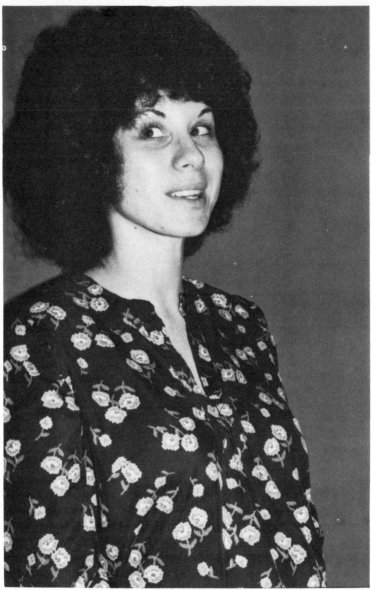

Judith Stein

MAXINE CHERNOFF

Maxine Chernoff, 24, has lived in Chicago all of her life. She co-edits *OINK!* magazine and has been published in *The Paris Review, Poetry Now, Unmuzzled Ox, Telephone, Out There, Center, The Wormwood Review,* and *Bartleby's Review.* She is married to poet Paul Hoover; they are the parents of Koren Eliza Hoover, born February 5, 1976.

AN ABRIDGED BESTIARY

for Peter Kostakis

As the story goes, Noah took animals of every variety aboard his famed ark. This, however, was not the case. The aardvark and the zebra were the only animals that the concise Noah allowed to join him. "Bears to yaks be damned," he shouted, when his wife asked permission for her pet monkey to board. Not recognizing in his single-mindedness the very quality that had endeared Noah to God, she smuggled the monkey onto the ship. This feat was easily accomplished, since Noah was extremely busy the forty days that the ship labored on the swollen sea. He was revising all known bestiaries, tearing out pages and tossing them overboard with the abandon of a crazed housewife cleaning out her refrigerator. By the end of the voyage he had written what he called *Noah's Book of Animals,* a two-page pamphlet praising the grace of the aardvark and the wit of the zebra.

Contrary to popular myth, it was the stowaway monkey and not the fabled dove, who announced the sighting of land. A strong swimmer, the monkey had followed the boat, collecting the pictures that Noah discarded. On the last day of the flood, Noah saw the pictures drying on a line suspended between two palm trees in the receding water. Amazed, Noah asked God what this portent could mean. God admonished Noah for his excessive frugality and blessed the intrepid monkey. The next morning all the animals were recreated, according to the discarded pictures that the monkey had saved for God.

THE DEAD LETTER OFFICE

Wistfulness covers the windows, like drapes. Ten men, armed with hankies, sort the mail into two categories: letters that make them happy, letters that make them sad. Don't get me wrong. These civil servants, trusted with the awesome duty of burning millions of letters a year, do not open the envelopes, like a mortician prying into the life of a client. It is the envelope itself that makes them sad: Childish handwriting scrawled to a deceased aunt makes them weep. A letter from overseas to a wife who has moved, unknown to her husband, creates such tumult that the walls quiver like jelly. Few letters are happy ones: the eviction notice never delivered, the lost bill. But when a happy letter does come into their possession, it's a red letter day. The men cheer wildly, tear up letters and toss them out of the window, ticker-tape fashion. And what bliss when something intervenes and a doomed letter, like the terminally ill patient, is saved.

THE SITTING

> "On November 8, 1875, W.C. Roentgen took a picture of his wife's hand. His mysterious rays became widely known by the mysterious letter X, but some of their significant properties became known only later. Meanwhile enterprising photographers established 'Roentgen studios' and did a lively business in x-ray sittings."

The line forms early each Sunday. Pregnant women bring their just-formed infants. Lovers are x-rayed in an embrace, creating a confusion of bone. One old man, wearing all black, says that he's come for a portrait of his hands, folded in death. A well-dressed family waits stiffly in line. The mother adjusts her daughter's ample ears as if they were taffy or branches of a bonsai tree. Men ogle the x-ray portrait labeled with the name of a well-known courtesan. "No two are alike," says the x-ray photographer. His thin, aesthetic hands hold up framed x-rays: "The men of the Academy. A dog who swallowed a key. A man milking his prize cow. The Queen Mother." Feathery shadows; even the fat lady is finely chiseled by the benevolent rays. As evening comes, the studio empties. The x-ray machine, nostalgic as a general on an empty battlefield, hums on into the night.

PAINTING

Each one of us has his own likes and dislikes, so do not think me rude if I say that I dislike certain types of painting. If your dislikes are not the same as mine, do not think that I am a minority of one.

In the first place I dislike those red paintings. Red does not look nice because the blood is also in red. That means red can represent blood. You never see a person who likes to see the blood.

Another type of painting I dislike is the black painting. It looks terrible, even the light black color. All the dirty things are almost in black. I am sure nobody would like to see or get the dirty things on his body or his stuff, like the coal, mice, devils, and a few others I cannot remember now. So you see a black painting is not a nice painting.

There are certain combinations of painting I dislike. I mean many different colors painting in one area. No matter how good the painting looks I think they look like the rubbish inside of the garbage can. If you open the garbage can you would see the stuffs in different dirty colors. I know no one would like to see the rubbish.

I dislike also those yellow paintings. That makes me sick. You know why? Because yellow can represent the death and the lack of nutritions. Like the plants before they die, first thing is they change from nice green to terrible yellow. The people also when they lack the nutritions. The surface of their skin changes to this terrible yellow. Now you may understand why I hate yellow painting.

There is another type dislike I remember, the white painting. When I studied in grammar school, I needed to wear white shirt, white shorts, white socks uniform. I was a neighbor boy. I liked to play the marbles with my friends after school, so all my white uniform sweep dirty on the ground. When I go home my mother saw that she was angry and hit me. Since that time I hate white color and swear never buy any more, neither white clothes nor white socks in my whole life.

And what type of painting do you like then? I sense this question coming from you, but I am not going to answer you, so, pray, excuse me.

FRED ASTAIRE

Ever since he danced on the ceiling in "Royal Wedding," he hasn't been the same. There is a longing, a profound blush, that starts in his toes and seizes the ankles. It is a feeling so intense that he must dash out of cabs, forgetting to tip his invisible tophat to passing ladies. Then, exhausted, he rests on a bench, feet tapping uncontrollably. Movies are impossible for Mr. Astair to attend. No sooner is he seated than he begins to turn objects upside down; popcorn rolls down the aisle, cokes splash like buckets of dirty water. During his last interview, Mr. Astaire turned his leather chair over and proceeded to straddle its broadmost part, as if riding a buffalo. His wife smiled knowingly. His little granddaughter ran in shouting "Grandpa! Grandpa! Pick me up!" Astaire took firm hold of the child's calves and held her like a double-handled mop, hair lightly brushing the ground. It is at moments like this that one sees an incredible transformation in Astaire's features. The deep wrinkles, engraved like monograms in fine silver, disappear. His blue eyes focus on the peak of his slanted roof and nestle there, like doves.

THE LAST AUROCH

Father wears antlers to dinner. Antlers so large that his head resembles a small tree in winter. We no longer look at each other, but just keep eating. Mother doesn't seem to notice it any more. She told us to treat Father as if nothing had happened. That was hard at first. So much had been in the papers. It was all they talked about in town. You see, Father destroyed the tourist trade. In fact, he destroyed the only commerce in town, other than cows: the museum where the last auroch was displayed. The last auroch, the ancestor of our modern cow, died in Poland in 1627. The people in that little town donated its bones and a few artifacts to our town as a goodwill gesture about 10 years ago. Because Father fought there in the war, they made him the curator of the museum. There he kept the bones in a glass case, the tarnished bell on the door, and the water trough and feed bag, always filled with cold water and the freshest alfalfa, in the middle of the room. Since there were no pictures of the auroch, we had to imagine how it looked: furrier and larger than our cows of today, with sadder eyes and a softer glance.

Father loved his job. He wouldn't have intentionally burned down that museum if his life depended on it. The fire started because he cared *too* much. When he'd come home Mother would ask if he'd had a good day. He'd always say that he had, that tourists had come, that he'd rung the auroch's bell for them. Nothing he said explained his drawn face and his red, swollen eyes. We could never understand his sadness until one night when we heard some commotion in the back yard. We all ran to the window and saw Father prancing around in the moonlight, wearing those huge antlers. It was a beautiful dance, a dance where Father expressed the longing that the last auroch must have felt for a companion. It was a mating dance, a dance that bulls in our county still do today. It went on until the sun came up.

Father never mentioned it to us. He'd come to breakfast looking drowsy and quietly leave for work. Soon he didn't even care about his uniform. His shirt was dirty. He lost buttons. The dance went on night after night. Soon he perfected a series of cries that went along with it. Pathetic mooing, guttural, low. Now Mother looked worn too. She was worried. One night there were two aurochs out in the back yard; Father, and Mother, wearing antlers somehow implanted in her hairdo. She copied his dance, but did it more demurely. She answered his calls in a voice so sweet that all of us nearly cried. In the middle of the dance, just at the point when it touched us most, something strange happened. Father screamed, "It's a lie! They aren't extinct! It's a lie!" He walked into the house and had his first sound sleep in weeks.

Father started going to work later and later. The museum suffered from his disinterest. One night a pile of old paper went up in flame. The museum burned before we could save the tarnished bell or a single bone. Since then Father doesn't speak to Mother any more. He won't take off his antlers and he won't even say the word "Cow." Sometimes I see him sending off letters. He addresses them to that town in Poland. Every day the mail comes. There is no reply. Every now and then he moos sadly, watching the tall grass swaying in the yard.

Mike Tappin

RICHARD FRIEDMAN

Richard Friedman was born in Chicago in 1951. College at University of Illinois Chicago Circle where Alternate University Poetry Collective met and the anthology *Jukebox Poems* was hatched. Since 1972, an editor of The Milk Quarterly and a director of The Yellow Press readings at The Body Politic. Author of two chapbooks *The Origin of Eyelids* and *21 Gun Salute*. *Straight* (Poems 1971-1975) was recently published by The Yellow Press. Employed as a mailman in Chicago from October 1973 to June 1975. From Jan. To April 1976, he taught the poetry workshop at Northeastern Illinois University. Active in Poets in the Schools program in Illinois and as moderator of weekly poetry radio shows on WZRD-FM and WBEZ-FM in Chicago.

RESIGNATION DAY

The slamming down of a badge
    on a desk or table proclaiming
                    "I QUIT!"

I can't be sheriff of this town no more
    I'm finished here
        I give up
    my employment my position my retirement fund
  my health benefits the free life insurance
the cost of living escalator clause

all abdicated, abandoned, renounced
           a subway ride downtown
      to re-sign on the dotted lines
of official forms
          "This was just my hobby"
I surrender, submit, & forsake
        this USPS rider's permit, operator's license, the silver
                                    star
rip the eagles off my shirts
    fly away w/letters in their beaks
  I relinquish their guardianship
        along w/the shine on my black shoes
    the rasp in my voice
              the 6 am circles under my eyes
That's right
    I'm leaving
  Here's formal notice in writing
Assume passive acceptance to the authority
           unresisting acquiescence to the right
of the mail to be delivered even tho I'm not there

AGAINST SOLIPSISM

    I'm all for the divine dispensations
Let them rain on me
      I'm Re-Zion & re: sign
  of a diminishing economic growth pattern

I'm through
              Call me UNEMPLOYED
                          no, self-employed
by the annulment of the government's
              Oath of Office
                          Pledge Allegiance Now To Thyself
       Civilian
                    Seniority Shattered
                                   an age of restoration
         Give me back my after midnights
My dawn as a sedative
                          my moon as a lamp face

                                          I'm back
              fishing for "letters in my head
                          now, not
                    in my hand"   (letter of resignation)

following the
                    steps along the San Clemente Beach
              of ex-Nixon
                          ex-Agnew
                    gimpily traversing the moors
                                          ex-Golda Meir
              ex-Khruschev
                          ex-Willie Mays

       ex-Thieu and the war dead of Vietnam

    but my last day was a triumph, a pleasure
I threw the same case
                    I'd started on
                    got the mail out on time

       fed my co-workers
                          & shook the collective hand
              of all assembled
                          to remain their fate

         mine to resign
                    but not w/o tears
                    for the friends left behind

                    & the identity obscured

    Now I'm just a man
            w/o prefixes
  a worker w/o a paycheck
                        a bed contains my tired head
        resting uneasy
                        for the ride west

Wagonmaster of my Soul
                    guide the wheels round
            may hands
                    of compasses & clocks
        register applause

                        these legs have just started walking

                this *poet*'s ready to roll

                    June 20, 1975

DARKNESS AT NOON

The zero vicinity
        reigns tonight in the city
    the light behind ice jeweled windows
        is just streetlight
    still the effect is
        dental x-rays, Eyptian tomb walls
    you can't see thru
    you being a slave
            condemned to die with The Pharoah
    we being compelled
            to awake at 2:00 AM
        to bend and scrape the green carpet

in homage to the janitor
providing uncustomary heat
at this hour
In the paper a man
commands me to write poems
that protest the bosses
is the janitor my boss?
True, his power over my
livelihood can be sudden & profound
lightning bolts ascending steam
& I'd rather his cigarette
on the bathroom floor
shaved head in the manner of a bearer
massive frame & viscious dog
were absent from me most days
but now I need him
and thank him for his service
technically I pay him
he is my employee
right, & Nixon, Ford & Daley
work for me
when they work, right?
still they never
call me boss
The Egyptians knew
"THE SUN IS THE BOSS"
Would I change this relationship?
Each light ray
is an order
with chemical kickbacks
built into the system
Are the clouds
of the ruling class?
must be, for w/o them
and the rain of their insistence
we'd die
There is a heirarchy
of atmospheric zones
layers of biosphere
we attack w/ our spray cans
Is this a struggle worth winning?
We're all workers

and write poetry
   as easy as plants
play their role
   given the necessary nourishment
sun & water
   food & shelter
a job and an allotment of money
This be our birthright
   Divisions like phylum
   can't tell me who's my brothers & sisters
Bosses work for someone too
   as the janitor works for the landlord
"Dear Landlord,
   Please don't put a price
      on my soul"
   our burden *is* heavy
     But we carry it together
   or there's a dent
     in the ground where it falls
Green, blue
    & earth
   rule this day
   yellow sun must
      have its way
But as a star
   our sun must die
   This solar system,
     universe & existence—
A Doomsday Machine in space

So human problems
   are not everybody's
    Tiny Pluto cherishes
   Big Sun's last
     weak signal
   more than our name
  for its roundness
   or our tracking of its orbit

There are things
   the Heavens do w/o
    thinking about them or

43

punching a time clock first
And as factory workers
let's face it:
men & women are best
at creating emotion
As I now am consumed
by love for my parents
my first bosses
Father dying now
w/Mother at his side
and sadness for their
fate that forecasts mine
and yours and ours
A race and planet
whose manifest destiny
is not California, but extinction
That knowledge terrifying
yet calming—It erases
hate & distinctions
between people for me
We stand together
as I see it
and I'm working
with anyone's help
who offers
to share
the pain & joy
of a life I'm
just beginning
to look at
on the edge
of a black hole
working to find
the steel hat that fits
with a sun ray
in its center
working to make
the spare in
my vest pocket
beat strong forever
awake to hear the heat
rise in the pipes

a poetry workers
and bosses understand
alike as they must be
and I work to protest
the misguided
Presidents & Ministers
Mayors & Cops
I protest
the injustice
of worlds within worlds
deprived of the goods
abandoned to starve
and I protest
the oppressors everywhere
Indira Ghandi, Idi Amin, Ian Smith
they know their names
& at home we
know the names too

And I protest
this life
while loving to live it
and celebrating
its power
To merge my life and art
before me the words
heatseeking &
delivering the message
that I cry
for us all
and listen to it all
awash in an ocean of light and sound
moving ahead
of myself
to meet my words
as they land
on the shore
of a mainland
where the sun
never sets
but is switched
off at night.

Mike Tappin

PAUL HOOVER

Paul Hoover serves currently as poet-in-residence at Columbia College, President of The Poetry Center at the Museum of Contemporary Art, and as co-editor, with Maxine Chernoff, of *OINK!*. Poems have appeared in *The Paris Review, Chelsea, The Iowa Review, Poetry Now,* and *New,* "among others." A collection of short and one-line poems, *Hairpin Turns,* was published by OINK! Press in, uh, 1972. "After poetry," Mr. Hoover says, "I take the most satisfaction from the numismatic study of developing nations, primarily those achieving nationhood after my own majority."

AFTER THE UNEXPECTED ANSWER (*Magritte*)

Because there was no camera
I punched a hole in the door,
a small hole in your form,
and stared at you through it.
It was easier to remember you then,
the whole room a camera, you were,
I believe, standing on your head.
Later I stared at pieces of paper, at floors,
waiting for you to appear, silhouette
notched like a key.
I placed my head on a tripod, and,
reaching under the skirt of hair,
adjusted a few cold knobs.
White empty tables surrounded my tongue;
one eye mechanically shuttered
quickly as a cell's lovelife.
I see you now when I wish.
Wearing shoes on your hands,
you bend at the waist, you stand,
shaking out your mouth's pockets.
Your image, like a slow bullet,
wobbles straight through me.
Suddenly I'm a drunken horse
stepping on softer soil with each hoof,
until even reason is maudlin
and a clown's reddest rage is only
a distant blur of greasepaint.
The pleasure of seeing through doors, love,
can't be improved on.
Stand still! Don't move,

as, trying to remember,
I strike myself in the chest like a typewriter
under a monkey's instructions.
This odd doll, memory of you,
sits in a corner, nudged by a finger of pain.
A bead of sweat, like a wheel,
breaking surface on its body.

A CIVIC AUTOBIOGRAPHY

How funny you are today, Chicago,
like Howard Keel in *Showboat*
singing to a dress form
or the acrobatic dwarf dressed as a star
announcing the big production number
in anything by Busby Berkeley,
though it is trite to praise him,
the dwarf, that is.
Staggering under tinfoil &
"the chains of disfigurement"
he runs between the showgirl's legs
smack into a door;
she shivering to remember her dream
of a blind date in bruised heaven,
he in top hat and tails,
face submerged like a fin as
"hairy bodies stamp on the fields"
of their affection. In the suburbs,

a good wife, ex-nun and mercenary,
wakes to the landscape of her bed,
a few hills fungusing the pillow,
a glittering lake propped between wrinkles
like a glass snail. And so,
she changes the sheets once more
without waking her husband
from his rotten well. The hills fall
with their cattle like yodels played
on a damp Victrola.
We smile to receive them. It reminds us of parades.
In the Loop, secretaries gaze from office windows,
their bodies already half confetti; snow falls
over the city like saccharine tablets,
the air plural, the Chagall blase.
Here, as spiders live, so do we,
clinging to the outside of high-rises,
one to a window, dazed as bulletholes
by the light of our feelings' false star.

THE ALARM CLOCK

I find it, weakly ticking, at the edge of the yard. It's the
cheap, round kind a day laborer, whose wife left him long ago,
uses to wake himself up in the morning. The casing is light
green plastic, a fact which causes the ticking to resonate fully, as
if it were emanating from the sound box of a guitar or a cave. It
is the sort of clock that in ringing might waddle across a dusty
dresser and fall into a drawer of luminous socks. The sort that
might escape, given half a chance.

I assume it has fallen from some window and rolled or crawled on its hands to this spot. Except for a grass stain and a little mud, it's in perfect condition. I consider also the Lassie variation: having been left in a motel by friendly vacationers, it is struggling cross country toward home. But how far? Five hundred, perhaps a thousand miles? I look in awe up and down the road, across the beanfields.

Frankly, I don't want to get involved. Picking it up, I throw it like a softball as far away as possible. It hovers for a moment at the peak of its parabola like a heartbeat over a ballpark. Then it falls with a pathetic little thump.

Now, back at the house, reading the paper, I begin to feel bad. I imagine it ringing all alone in a ditch like a bum having a nightmare. Worse yet, the pathetic running down. The evening edition scattering behind me, I run down the road, hands in the air at ten and two. Already, I see, it has moved halfway back to the house, spinning on its face in advancing circles. *Here you are,* I say, plucking it from the weeds like a sputtering child from a green lake.

Later we sit on the front porch in silent companionship. Its flat pugilist's face reveals little of its feelings, reminds me of Leo Gorcey staring at fireflies. I know there is something black in its past. I can smell anger.

In the morning, I resolve, I'll drive it to my sister's house in the next county. She has an attic with a cot and a small round window, the perfect hiding place. From the window it will at least be able to see the garden: metallic cabbages, listless corn, beans clutching their way over the fence.

Soon it is beside me on the seat of the pickup, facing forward. We're bouncing along a dirt road, the dust not yet rising high because of the early morning dew. I realize suddenly I could be Warren Oates in BRING ME THE HEAD OF AL-FREDO GARCIA, chatting guiltily with the rider beside him.

A police siren, like the sun coming up, rings and whines its way nearer from somewhere up the road.

THE FUTURE OF THE FISHBOWL

A woman gives birth
to a ball of glass.
Soon afterwards,
the nurse hands it to her
wrapped in a blanket.
Part of it protrudes, like a cheek.
She admires it for a while,
then the nurse carries it to the crib
the way a lobster carries a lightbulb.
Later, while the other patients are sleeping,
the mother sneaks into the nursery
and, leaning over the crib,
shines a flashlight through her child.
The scenes of its future life
splashing around the room
like roller rink lights. . . .

DEPRESSION ODE (11/23/75)

Born in the heart of the Institute,
a child sits in its father's hand
with a sweet smile, dreaming of Chihuahuas.
This is far from the truth.
A door opens in the hallway of a pencil.
Behind another, a watchdog sleeps inside a bottle
like its own saddest meal. Well!
It eats only swans, and the old professor,

double-exposed, hurts his white heart.
Taking to bed alone,
he switches off the electric fence,
its hum fading like a shrug.
The floodlights are merely hankies
collapsed over tall poles, though one,
one is a spinning plate no one
rushed to tend. It wobbles.
It is enough to say "disappointment,"
for all over the complex,
as in a black harmonica,
silence butts the walls
of its rooms and cages
and will not settle down.

FOR ISIDORE DUCASSE

The notes of schoolmates
who knew you only casually
proved valuable: "His young headache,
punctuated by piano chords,
cut 88 roads through an ossuary..."
while in your heart something heavy and hairy,
with a broad back, bruised the walls it leaned on.
Sometimes, to gather your thoughts,
you fired a pistol across a green park.
The crowds would gather into childish patterns,
as if a magnet were passing over.

Words were occasionally formed,
often misspelled, the letters large and simple.
You traced them with a finger,
breaking a window of air
with your hard flea's head.
"A" came up *A*, electric.
"B" was trundled in on wheels.
"C" leveled the glorious harvest.
"D" broke up in the rapids.
"E" fell through your hair.
"F" was twice deadly.
"G" caused the wagon to spill,
while "H", thinking the mirror logical,
often stood in front of it.
Behind each bullet, actual doors closed.
Someone was hired to do this,
but the pay was low, the hours long,
and the uniforms expensive.
It was a difficult time. . .
and your room darkened from the top and sides
like the end of a silent movie.
There wasn't an audience, yet
I would like to say, even today,
I hear your voice in every recording
a dog makes with its upper incisors.
But it wouldn't be so.
Instead, I see:

> your feet, as "M" leaps from a building.
> your arms, when "T" carries water to the fields.
> your legs, if "R," Victorian, wears her skirts too long.

The truth is, you were always seated at the piano,
and the love you wanted, like an acrobat,

hung by its heels. To keep the time,
your clumsy pedal foot danced beside its pale brother,
which of course tied itself to a string
some dark evening.

Mike Tappin

ANGELA JACKSON

Angela Jackson was born in 1951 in Jackson, Mississippi. She is a member of the Organization of Black Culture and an editor of Nommo magazine. Author of *Voo Doo/Love Magic* (Third World Press). She is a winner of the Conrad Kent Rivers Memorial Award from Black World magazine and active in The Illinois Arts Council Poets in the Schools Program.

BASEMENTMUSIC: THE LOVE AFFAIR

burn me mellow
deep
blue into brown
body
baby
leave on the basement music
hush my mouth in the shadow of your
afro
glow
call
me
incredible crazy lady
thick
honeylips heavyrich with sounds saved for you
hungry hungry basement music
way
within
within
flooded
with
summer
sweatwinesmoke
say
me a midnite set
where
syrup grind
sugar
these
ole
eyes is dusty discs

been thru
&aroun
turnin
on no groove

bend into this slow drag
chicago-walk
swaystride
coolwarm
as summer hawk
lazy
fling my body against yours
cradle/d
casual
grace
baby
i'm amazing
myself&
maybe
you
too?

turn me deep
mellow
like cigarette fire
a
spear
spark
in the dark
burnsoft
no more hurting nights
of
never

hush my hungrymouth in the shadow
of
your
afro
glow
call
me
incredible
incredible crazy lady
lavish
o
lush in your love
throw your arms around me. . . . . . .

FOR OUR RISING (WARRENSSONG)

with your
       foldedvoice
with your
       creased/eyes
with your
       spindling spine
with the melodies of your jazz

brother
now
you stoop
to
scoop
the last remaining grains
from
the fallowingfields
where

you
have cottoned the noise of your carnage
where you have
oil/d
the soils
with your broken sweat
where
you cave
the corroding clays
in your palms
and breathe against the encroaching crusts

we
knead for bread

thru
the bloodwashed glasses
still
remembered shadows stripping the lingering longgrasses
of your gait
i have seen you thru
these
streets a stream of ash and incipientflower
stalking
where you bloom the lastgods
the last beads of maize
and rose
i have seen you
sister
say that this is so

with your
            foldedvoice
with your
            creased/eyes
with your constantly
            cradling loins
with the melodies of your raining songs
sister
thru these streets of recoiling eyes & perpetualloss
&chaos
brother
with this dance of sinewing hands

trust the earth to bear
greater than despair

FROM A
SPEECH DELIVERED IN FREEDOM HALL
ON AFRIKAN LIBERATION DAY:
WORDS FROM A WELFARE MOTHER

the
president
is a welfare-chiseler

he
chips away my sons life
scale
his years
like flakes from fish

cluttering the kitchen floor
with tears

a
professional
welfare-chiseler

nonchalant
certified

public
faring well
atop my breath-taxed
centurychiseled
illegitimate cherished
children

he flush my daughters
futures

down the clinic toilet

he forge my name
   peel out her womb

he pee on my preciousseeds

the
president
is a welfare-chiseler

representative of the common
good
he got a long/strongarm
reaching musclelaw

way up in my neighborhood
he pay no income tax.

the
president
is a welfare-chiseler

he
chip away my sons life
scale
his years
like flakes from fish

cluttering my kitchen floor
with tears

Mike Tappin

HENRY KANABUS

Henry Kanabus was born on the 25th of February, 1949 in Amberg, Germany. Lived in Valley, Washington near the city of Spokane for five years. Attended Northeastern Illinois University. Studied with Ed Dorn, Ted Berrigan and Tom Raworth. An organizer of The Blue Store Readings 1971-72. Co-editor of *Stone Wind* magazine (sole editor of issue #5). Published in numerous magazines including: *The World, Telephone, The Milk Quarterly, Stone Wind, Buffalo Stamps, Chicago* and *Mati*. Winner of the Illinois Arts Council Award for poetry in 1975. Books: *Flood Lights/ Poems 1971-1973* (Apocalypse Publications 1975); *Particles of Violence/ Poems 1973-1975* (unpublished); *Tits of Callisto/ An Erotic Science Fiction Novel* (unpublished). "Current occupation: Poet and Foreigner."

THE BEARDSLEY FLESH

I

This lady has a special
    interest
let us follow her
she sees

a masked dance

do you see her
hooved foot
pirouette

There is another
with a spotted dress

Her hand behind her
gives the sign
    of satan

We can tremble now
her eyes dart

One can see her face
chiseled like ice
in the curtain

There is two of them
both women.

II

Her dress billows

She is standing
at the entrance of the forest

the boy white flower
amuses her temperament

There are petals
on the hands
of the infant.

III

His cape is marvelous

a sheet of flame
white orchids

Wings on the ankles
of his feet pointed

What a cruel accident

she prays obviously
Wealth and the dwarf
make a lewd exit.

I have noticed suddenly
the feet of the altar
are goat feet.

IV

Messalina walks
with her breasts outrageous.

V

Atalanta is a huntress.

VI

A word is written
      on a leaflet
She touches
her self

VII

A child carries
the gallows

a silhouette.

THE DAY BIRTH PLACARD (for Amy)

December and the settling heart remain
in collusion after all
        these years have taught them
nothing
but witholding time
Pensive the skin is   Alive
        and the wearisome mind
        refrains from joy
You have held me for an instant
on the green sofa on the machine
                sofa on toy house
holds I have come
to love you as the winter
grows its long hands

And it is not that serious not that
cornering glance
                you have given
promises I build on joyously
mistaking harmonies of chance
                I am strung by
trinkets of violence   Jealousy
and hunger skin
        You feed them
        ampules of fine verbiage
and sadden to see them
rise with the mourning wind.

SONG (THE WREN)

How the rose lays on
     your shoulder
the water sways
beneath you

Light hits your face

The leaves
surround you
I tell I love you

Lights hits your face.

MARGIE SILVER

Oil wells and blue narcissus brighter than an oak leaf.
Fancy that on hiller miner overcast. Sunday morning.
     Orange pony smaller than a mule twice ugly. Margie Silver
whore and opium hole. Daughter of Montgomery.
     "Best he lick that cactus flower afore my honey. Cast an
eye on mission hill, lil' pony."
     Hoof the dust, the collar bones of dogs, ribs of desert
monkeys. Rain this side of Bootlove Kansas turns to vapor
'bove the clouds. Stones and mountains cover half the country.
     "Best he love a widow spider afore he touch my money.
Sniff the air, orange pony. Does he love me?"

     Night and shadows, eyes the red of iron blazing. Smoke
as sweet as China fields. Margie Silver sleeps like deep water.

STILL LIFE

Many people watch the fire

It is burning now

a weeping child

now a banister

Through a window

leaps a nude

with a hammer.

MANDY AS NIGHT BOUQUET

Fine rings of silver dangle
from her face   The circle
white as light porcelain
nipples
                culminate in fire
forests of cunt bramble
etching silk processions
on his face

Her mouth apologies
casual in winter
shoulder slight illusion
        of anger linked with
grace enchanted
rain

Sentient her fragrance   tactile
as morning fog her fragrance
metrical   as morning fog her fragrance
came

THE PLEASANT EVENING

Consider your intellect
a prestigious lump of meat
set in liquid

It wallows like a fetus
in your forehead
seeps into your eye
your shoddy toolshed
plays dead

Take your time
as you take your woman

drink your wine
and smoke a cigarette

My cock stands
at the drop of a g-string

Our love bends
like the wings of a robin.

THE BRITTLE EYE

Yes and you know
that red sky. . . the rind
of it over street shoulders
gives with neon insistence
a violet gaze   blue windows

The troubled cloud
winds with the river
    White wisps escape

like prominences
leaving the sun

And yet after years
after the rain meant
    only rain
I take from day the wistful
promise. . . spoken by her
realized by your permanence

In the evening of bewilderment
hold me
You pertain.

THE CENTAPOD

It being lost
the arraignment being
lost to him

He sorrows in a field of
    ugly tits

The arraignment being lost
it being lost to him

He is injured in the wire
    of her barking cunt
    welded to his tongue

It being lost
the arraignment being
lost to him

He hungers at the gates
    of maniacal need

The arraignment being
lost it being
lost to him

She has outlawed joy
    retracting the blue
    eyes he has found

It being lost
the arraignment being
lost to him.

FURNACE MONKEY

The furnace monkey
sleeps in basements

peddles toothpicks
loves his shotgun

He stole the windows
from your stairway

sold the wood work
kept the glass

for your namesake.

Gerard Malanga

PETER KOSTAKIS

Peter Kostakis, architect of the AACM (Association for the Advancement of Creative Musicians) Circle campus debut in form of a Muhal Richard Abrams Sextet concert, took his M.A. at UICC in 1975. Ranched out his spare time as Body Politic Series of Monday Night Poetry Readings co-director and graphic artist, later as Poetry Center board member; since 1972, as co-editor of *The Milk Quarterly*/The Yellow Press. One OP book, *Sweet Little Sixteen* (Music Poems 1973); *The Ministry of Me* is unpublished. 1975 trip to Greece. Bestiarist, and chief of Animal Antics Unit. Age 24: has been the subject of many poems.

THE GALLERIES

for Frank O'Hara

1

Am I to become profligate?
In an 8 x 8 x 8 glass cube this does not seem likely
There is no room for shyness
No time for the advantages of reading Sade
My eyes are a pair of dice

2

Boxcars

3

I have to take off my shoe to pull up the sock.
As I do, I am afraid Marcel Duchamp
will sneak a spout in my mouth
to let in plaster of Paris
by the gallon

4

What is profligate?
Krazy Kat on the ritz
A canary in a sixteen track studio

5

I sign Frank's name in a guest ledger
"We're dilettantes," I tell the guy
in the melting plaid suit

6

The little girl in Hans Bellmer
tugs the skin on either side of her belly
full tight in the air like drapery, or a sail.
She is placid as she

surveys the blueberries inside,
erasing the bounds of her reason
with the blink of an eye
the way they do in Arabia

7

St. Theresa used her skin as a sail to reach God
I use my eyes to deal in an unsociable game
I see you too and raise you three
Guess who is the gambler of this poem?

8

Book in the stainless steel cabinet I admire
your tenacity, although there is a hole in you.
Holes admit of air, and so do I.
In me they develop feverishly
My friend the time has arrived for frankness
By blood I am an aristocrat
I live in my house
Air changes blue to red
I get angry when I cut myself
and find out who I am
That is decidedly not a form of Zen
a bow at the Seine in the form of dolphins
Blue blood is neither of these things

9

The domestic iron erect with nails
multiplies an Irishman's third leg
to the third power—not what he intended.
Do not volunteer your trousers to the housewife
with the armored sex

10

Doors bend in a Chinese way
naive beneath calligraphy
as the stork ferries a baby past
couched in his beak of feathers.

Gaining entrance, I will become
a forgotten style
a Ming period hand that is languid

11

What objets d'art we are!
Pipe cleaner here, coiling there for arteries.
The sponge assures intelligence,
which is the eating of bread or
volition for the man whose desire to eat bread demands
and receives adequate publicity throughout the body.
Gourmets regard eating as an art
Gastronomically they are correct
The swallow distinguishes itself as not one but many
complicated birds executing dives in their gullets

12

There is always the danger
a Peoples Gas man will put his baloney
on the painted bread

THE BLACK SWAN

It was during the winter of 1870, at the Lake of
Swans, in Mississippi, that the patient was hunting at
night, in a small boat and by the light of torches. In the
course of their maneuvers a flock of Swans was suddenly
encountered which took to flight without regard to any-
thing that might be in the way. As the man raised his
arm instinctively to ward off the swiftly rising birds, he
was struck on his forearm by the wing of one of the
Swans in the act of getting under motion, and as the
action and labor of lifting itself were very great, the
arm was badly broken.

SIRIUS, A DOG STAR

for Barry Schechter

1

These animals, it was said, were not ordinary animals: they were professional animals battling before human spectators in warehouses of outlying districts.

One must witness the symphony of an evening, by dying light expunged gradually to shadow—its mouth irised—a vowel-yellow "o" at center, dead center, of the pit; dissonant howls; infernal grunts; a sudden feint to the left upending to the right; hideous punctures upon the fraction-of-a-second-late thorax; at nothing, lunges blinded by streams of blood; innumerable evasions and variations on the above; then, inevitably, the crescendo spring of the kill, coda of welts and scars and the canine unchaining of soul from body until legs kick no more. There are few events that match for grandeur a dogfight well managed and respectfully arranged.

Sirius had been gaining ground in the league. The pointed ears prompted conversation, as did his lightning backside. Spectators reminded themselves how man had domesticated first the horse, after that the shoe, the hat and now "Sirius the Dog Star," a credit to his master and to his kind.

2

Skirting the huge drums, dodging omnipresent workman's booms hanging like Spanish moss from the rafters, I enter the fight area and see a faded tarpaulin unceremoniously lugged from the center of a room awash with cigarette smoke, revealing a steep indentation of the warehouse floor. I manage a path to the front. Behind an illuminated screen shadows writhe in livid turmoil, the soulless motion of ghosts, or decals clenching for surface, or fanblades fighting to the death! Sirius is someone's hand gone tired, a phonograph record whose fluctuations of loudness jostle my ears to attention!

CALYPSO FOR COMMITTED MEN

"Great Black Music" means
you have to listen to it
in the dark, as I do now

cleansing rite and when it's played
say, see the body aura'd from above
x-rayed, your skeleton

with juice on, tubed white neon
like hands up in the dark.
It takes the stand

Muhal's staunch green Alpine
hat which floats above piano
which is brainchild of harp

(and isn't that what I write about?)
presides over a scintillating
left alone glissando

is eternal gliss you have to listen to
in the dark and the piece of wood
that bites is Malachi's trust

meets fingers biting back
the way prides of lions play.
Here is a speed that picks up

the weight of the world
with frantic delicate claws:
A.A.C.M. a cub at ten years

specimen, the life of spice

10 December, 1975

SO JAH SEH

In my country life goes
to a party, then empties
like a museum exit
beset by shriners.

Once someone yelled
"Look!", but still
I missed two kittens
swept in the pail

by a passing storm,
and it was boiling
water they fell into
just as now I forget

how we entertain in my
country, how the moist
beautiful heart is torn
by an anchor making a

mistake. My cousin and I,
in the early days of
my country, impersonated
foreigners. A youngster

I pretended to be
in line just to push
people. Today I crack
the combination of an

embrace and low "Love!"
repeatedly to boulders
pale before caves to find
lost buttons from greatcoat.

LINES TO NEFERTITI

Wasn't I stupid to assume
constants in life, constant life:
like now, my eyes dumbly trail

the length of a leash, light;
my blood, sleepless, paces the perimeter
of a shoreline,

as I consider the dead within
adrift pale autos, mod style
Vikings in the expressway night.

Then I get to testing my coffin, color
too loud, lines too sleek
(how can a self sail away?)

I remember First Cemetery of Athens,
how the sculptor dropped dead
noticing a life intense

likeness in his own sepulchral
statue of a young woman;
the stone of Seferis was a ship

plain marble like your average
millionaire's; while at the burial place
of poet Palamas's little boy

the father's inscription moved
me to record, "too bad a kid
washes up in the hereafter,

too/his dad earnestly implores
someone comb his hair there."
So Beauty can be, as in horror

legends, "beyond the grave."
I know, because a postcard Nefertiti's
cheekbones clang

81

(by Thutmose, 18th dynasty)
in my head, cut thought
off its tracks, there too

the sound of Beauty's sandals
be clacking over floors
in temporal retreat if not

extinction. She winsome she
lissome she win some she
lose some and she's installed

lines of affection in my skull.
The phone's a bone
torn from the ligament of love

and I'm the party wired to please.
"Operator, connect me with those
above to tell me what it's like."

THE CRAYFISH

The crayfish is a sort of harpsichord, a love affair
of the line given lasting expression: armorial, the bone
that achieved miracles by trysting with a mirror and
looking at an echo: the crayfish is a fixed idea. With the
deepest dish, noiseless, it rhymes, silence its favorite
song. A self-flattering practice among them consists of
using the pincer to strike a penny against their cold
brown segments, and so hear truth resound. The cray-
fish is a sort of harpsichord, rusting in water.

Judith Stein

ART LANGE

Art Lange was born and raised in Chicago, graduated from Northeastern Illinois University (B.A., 1973) and southern Illinois University (M.A., 1974). Organized *ad hoc* poetry reading series at UNI 1972-73. Illinois Arts Council Award winner for poetry published in 1975. Editor of *Brilliant Corners* (a magazine of the arts). Author of *On Impulse* (a *ditto-rations* chapbook). Works also appeared in *Brilliant Corners, Buffalo Stamps, Chicago, Here It Is, Mati, The Milk Quarterly, No Name, OINK!, Out There, Stone Wind*, etc.

COPENHAGEN

It is a privilege to see so much confusion.
An opaque illusion
"The visitor dare never fully speak at home
for fear of being stoned
as an imposter." Clearly defined pseudopodia.
Ghosts
       "telling me my own dream"
arrive to arrive and to arrive here in such thick

"Disobedient persons being summarily removed
and not allowed to return without permission in writing."

must avoids:
a closing of eyes   seldom successes
and complaisancies
described by the cartographer of 1539.

We should like to know how that was done.

The work of careful men with shovels.

TO MYSELF

"flocculations of cirrus hang" morose
and slovenly
glistening wet amid dense grey
panels of daylight spending
black hours over an unclean
line dreaming
black and lovely labyrinths

A LANDSCAPE BY CEZANNE

skylights purse red roofs in shallow
cubes skin brightly crossed
and lofty
lively light will pose unlacing

an air an every sexy self
thing like unfleshed often constant
green around gone briefly spellbound
bending supporting the shapes they fade

FOR PEE WEE

A paucity is gathering at the real places
in variations of (past) miracles
                              recognitions
after the events of
                    dawn dark slow rain
comes flying away
looking absolutely melancholy w/ leisure
content if minor forms appear
within the narrow time when veils dissolve
                                    and disappear
in this rare place
intonation as lace
                    network small white preparations
into a view
of rich high levels of random new saliences of feature
as
suddenly huge the whole uplifting moon
but there is no greater love

HOMAGE TO HANS HOFMANN

Verb
of what's warm in an itch
    abundance
    an unruly tangle
but you verb in the stretching
    begins
clean surfaces and this flash
    and tiny figures floating in it
a green wash
    gone gaudily a bloom of grey
       swayed
into probability like a wall
and
a
sign   HOW TO KEEP IT WARM
late afternoons are the *worst*
    as
    obvious
    as
    an elbow
and against undulance of again literal calmness
peeling
and freezing and thawing
out
  absorbed and shocked into a sense of serious joy
in the liquidly
cloister
the rectangular yellows
stupidly splinter and pound for the duration
yellow yellow
    stretch vague in it but catch
up
on
sleep
inside a light bulb
    the horizontal greens of expecting
      a
      telegram
takes on punctuation

                                 flashes like troughs of oleo

in

windows   rip

                         the fewer faked

                                   rather bright

green grey in hue a few quick step
is inevitable ripens blur blue and merge
the nerve
            the corner
                   painted edges
                   of curbs
come clear to calm constellations
and chase
and radiance
and velocity

TRUST

It takes a long
time to hear and
then you cannot put

it into words.
These things are not
limitless. The sly brim

covers the lying
eyes. Too clever, with
wide smiles actually

bacteria. Ultimately
you will be saturated
with starlight. It's

a complication.

NYC

The air is green
          loud morning
the streets are turning within their colors
various others
          bitter the air
covertly cover   phrase over phrase
fields of flutter flutter pages consecutively
twist
      and the heat's on
             a sweet rain
                  treacle
                  obfuscation
(I'm) well acquainted w/ confusion
I move towards it haggardly
           a hard intonation of with the slowly and the
flaps in a circle of lives and extension
               conclusively
dreaming in marble
          of the (dark) w/ meteors
                a formal spasm
placid obscure palpable
          several silver shapes
whose least amazing characteristic is
            it may not always be so
fragile
windows go
       (orange) in the slowly
            shy lurch small invitingly
imperceptible
       and impersonates a street
             sneers
above eloquent air awakens form
          bare
putting it mildly
pulverizing
       fresh arrangements
           esurient
             prostrate and amazed
who comes is occupied

                slippery intense witty huge
you
    were sight given permission
              meant to mention
(breathless w/ sharp necessary droll)
             the myth
whiteness and whose shape remains sharp as a syllable
vague and insistent
        propitious while
waiting carves out for them a giddy insomnia
engraved is sheer face
        contradiction
             simultaneous windows
mysterious w/ gaslight
        bright sky bright sky
so odd and light and dry

RUPTURED MELODIES

The sound
        then a soft halo around it
an essential caustic rigor reached
             lifted aloft (a still softer
continual process of obtaining
        such elegant streaky lines in brocade)
like the shade aggressively reflected
    off the molding wall arch and paraphernalia
and it's a gradual dissolution of lines of light
        (feathers of light in fact)
or rather angles
stands as a kind of dancing partner for the memory
        in a great sudden spurt of shadow
w/ no visible means of support
          as the notes sound bouncing
off the light or lack of it under the arches of a
soporiferous baroque cathedral

Kofi Moyo

HAKI R. MADHUBUTI (DON L. LEE)

Haki R. Madhubuti (Don L. Lee), born February 1942, was raised on Detroit's lower east side and educated at Wilson Junior College and Roosevelt University in Chicago. In 1967 his first poetry collection, *Think Black*, was privately printed (to be republished the next year by Broadside Press). Later titles include: *Directionscore*, *We Walk the Way of the New World* and *Book of Life*. He helped institute the Writer's Workshop of the Organization of Black American Culture, and he initiated the Third World Press. Currently he teaches at Howard University (Washington, D.C.) and directs the Institute of Positive Education.

WE WALK THE WAY OF THE NEW WORLD

1.

we run the dangercourse.
the way of the stocking caps & murray's grease.
(if u is modern u used duke greaseless hair pomade)
jo jo was modern/ an international nigger
           born: jan. 1, 1863 in new york, mississippi.
his mommo was mo militant than he was/ is
jo jo bes no instant negro
his development took all of 106 years
& he was the first to be stamped "made in USA"
where he arrived bow-legged a curve ahead of the 20th
      century's new weapon: television.
which invented, "how to win and influence people"
& gave jo jo his how/ ever look: however u want me.

we discovered that with the right brand of cigarettes
that one, with his best girl,
cd skip thru grassy fields in living color
& in slow-motion: Caution: niggers, cigarette smoking
          will kill u & yr/ health.
& that the breakfast of champions is: blackeyed peas & rice.
& that God is dead & Jesus is black and last seen on 63rd
      street in a gold & black dashiki, sitting in a pink
      hog speaking swahili with a pig-latin accent.
& that integration and coalition are synonymous,
& that the only thing that really mattered was:
     who could get the highest on the least or how to expand
     & break one's mind.

in the coming world
new prizes are
to be given

we *ran* the dangercourse.
now, it's a silent walk/ a careful eye
jo jo is there
to his mother he is unknown
(she accepted with a newlook: what wd u do if someone
     loved u?)

jo jo is back
& he will catch all the new jo jo's as they wander in & out
and with a fan-like whisper say: you ain't no
                              tourist
                              and Harlem ain't for
                              sight-seeing, brother.

2.

Start with the itch and there will be no scratch. Study
     yourself.
Watch yr/ every movement as u skip thru-out the southside of
     chicago.
be hip to yr/ actions.

our dreams are realities
traveling the nature-way.
we meet them
at the apex of their utmost
meanings/ means;
we walk in cleanliness
down state st/ or Fifth Ave.
& wicked apartment buildings shake
as their windows announce our presence
as we jump into the interior
& cut the day's evil away.

We walk in cleanliness
the newness of it all
becomes us
our women listen to us
and learn.
We teach our children thru
our actions.

We'll become owners of the   New World
the New World.
will run it as unowners
for
we will live in it too
& will want to be remembered
as   realpeople.

POSITIVE MOVEMENT
WILL BE DIFFICULT
BUT NECESSARY

(for John O. Killens)

remember past ugly to memories of the *once*
to memories of the used to be
lost days of glory, the forgotten-forgiven history of the race:
when sun mattered and the night was for sleeping
and not for planning the
death of enemies.

beautiful
realpretty like morning vegetation
beautiful
like Afrikanwomen bathing in Tanzanian sun
beautiful a word now used exclusively to describe the
                ungettable
            a word used to describe roaches disguised as
                people that viciously misrule the world.
times is hard rufus & they gointa be harda
come on champ   chop chop
hit hard   hit harda   catch up   chop chop
sleep less   eat right   rise earlier
whip dust into the eyes of excuse makers
talk to yr children about meaning,
talk to yr children about working for the race.
chop chop   hit hard   hit harda
beat it   beat it   beat it   now

in this world
we face our coming as hip slaves unknown to ourselves
unknown to the actual challenges of the race
do you know yr real name?
do you know the real reasons you are here?
check the smiles on yr enemies' faces
if you can identify yr enemies
they crawl from the earth in many faces: negroes,
militants, revolutionary integrationists, soul-brother
number 15, black capitalists, colored politicians
and pig-eaters lying about their diets.

listen now listen
open yr ears we got a number for you
listen, somebody is trying to tell us something,
listen, somebody is trying to pull our minds.
it ain't magic we be better if it will listen
let the words seek greater levels of meaning
split in there   words be   beat it   beat it words
beat it   now
it ain't gypsy tales or trails
or false eyes frontin for the devil
it ain't about the happy ending of the west
unless you are reading the future wrong.

listen, no doubt you're very smart
we can tell by the size of yr feet that you dance too
doin the kneeknot best in the land also a
fashionplate always very very clean
pink on pink in pink by pink runnin hard
no doubt you're the best athlete to confront
the 20th century since beaver bill
expert ping pong player for the state department.
we're still runnin bases in the blind
& only see money loves money a money lover
but
can you change the direction of the fog with money?
can you beat the deathmakers with money?
can you be respected as a man with money?
can you beat yr momma's rapist with money?
they ready to be beat   cause
it ain't about making you a star
hanging in space reciting "art"
it ain't about becoming better flesheaters
sharpening yr teeth on yr children's future
it ain't about becoming successful actors
black faced draculas & 007's disguised as life.

listen now, listen
fighters fight   that is what they do
come on champ   chop chop   hit hard   hit harda
catch up box yourself into meaningness
fighters fight while others watch & take the jobs.
talk to yr children about meaning

kill those comic books.
talk to yr children about working for the race
outlaw television.
start a battle for yr own mind.
this is it   this is it   is in   beat it   be
got you beat   if we be the best   better than most
there is to be   got to be, got to be, got to be
better than the best to beat the beast.

quiet world we are the people
summer's sun seen us through many winters
here son but we're stronger now   still
unseen unwanted now   we gather our thoughts now
clear our heads now   collecting our direction now
looking closer into eachother's eyes   now
seeing identity from doers now
looking toward the people that do now
getting as serious about our enemies
as we are about his holidays now   avoiding deathtraps now
observe Bobo studying the history of the race
it is difficult but necessary.
check Willa Mae giving time to the community school
it is difficult but necessary.
much of what is needed will be difficult but necessary
much of what is needed will be difficult but necessary

the truest men are sane men
who met and conquered madness about 40 or 50
years ago. we called them crazy then, we called
them "madmen from the east,"
they wanted to reshape our destiny,
they wanted to refocus our way of life.
we called them "madmen from the east."
they had strange names, ate funny meals,
didn't wear $300 suits or drive $10,000 cars
or sell their mommas for the leisure of the west.
these "madmen from the east"
confronted the real laziness of our ways,
forced us to take sides,
forced us to deal with ideas & concepts of living,
forced us to work for the people of the summer's sun.

much of what we must do
will be different from the west
will be different from the frozen impersonal west
will be different from the snow filled west
will be different from the gray concrete colors of the west.
got to be different
got to be   got got to be   got to be   beat it now
got to be different from   got to be   got got to be
different from the west   got to be   got got to be
different from the west
if we prize life itself   living
much of what we do will be difficult and different
will be difficult,
will be very difficult,
but necessary.

Mike Tappin

ALICE NOTLEY

Alice Notley was born November 8, 1945. Grew up in Needles, California. B.A. from Barnard College (NYC); M.F.A. from University of Iowa (Iowa City). 1 husband (Ted Berrigan), 2 children (Anselm & Edmund). Books include *165 Meeting House Lane* (anthologized in ALL STARS), *Phoebe Light, Incidentals in The Day World, For Frank O'Hara's Birthday. Alice Ordered Me to Be Made* (Poems 1975) will be published by The Yellow Press.

30TH BIRTHDAY

May I never be afraid
                especially of myself
                                but
Muhammed Ali are you telling
the truth?
                Well you're being true aren't you and
you talk so wonderfully in your body
                that protects you with physique of voice
        raps within dance
                                May I never be afraid

                rocked and quaked
                                        the mantilla is lace
                                        whose black is oak
But if I'm dark I'm strong
                        as my own darkness
my strength the universe
                        whose blackness is air
                        only starry
                        lace
But if I'm alive I'm strong
                        as life
Strong as the violets
in Marlon Brando's fist
                his dissemblance flourished into truth
                                                        She
took them
I'd take me too
                I do
        and my Ali I see you
                                a hard bright speck of me
the savage formalist
                authentic deed of gossip
        a kind body

101

"THE VIRTUE OF UNCREATEDNESS"

?

immediately create

Roses beautiful
        when I look at you
your leaves against
what a lightful and formal baby-
    blue volkswagen!
             touches the roses
   in the window plane
     though one street width away

What is watching? A

    peddlar of insects
    a figure, possibly god impersonator
    a rain charm probably
    a flowers music dance
    a slit-drum head
    a kneeling figure, figuratively,
        from Duck River, Mississippi
    "I'm in my sin"
    a standing figure fetish
    a funerary hood
    wood paint nails cloth leather beads shells
    arrows twine nuts
    a Maiden spirit mask

        totally uncreated!

      Here

take this mess it's yours it falls away into

A silver truck just drove into, and stopped,
      the entire window

           falls away into
                  dot dot dot

      Dot Lamour
      Dot in Oz
      Dot Parker.

TO WCW

The shape of my second son's head—
the beauty of the line and of the
father
    there—
        that
it is the male principle?
           that the prince
enables me to be kind

           the prince is he who
swam naked at night in winter ocean the king
was a constellation the male

           plays for death and it
it is a draftsman's head
           life, a perfection I
don't live for the form of
           but love so my
son's form—he of my kind whose line
will be apparent to me
           my line I
              as I tell

Alice Notley

TRANSLATION OF A CHINESE TRIBUTE TO JADE

I believe in the uncarved block and my dark
envelopment
              with the street construction worker
the Holy Ghost
              perfectly abrasive
                  in ruby dust paste
              impenetrable in flowers
              bursting forth to give all of itself
                  from human faces though it can't be
spent I believe in pregnancy and childbirth and yelling
      at your kids and at the evil in you and the
          humiliation and actual absence of it and the strength
              got therefrom
                  to keep yelling and bursting with light
so you can love your husband all in one
"the well of pure water that appears mysteriously
              without boring"
I hate saviours I love heroes
                          the older artists of the
                          messy lives
moss entangled in melting snow
jade rests might
          amuse the writer's wrists
I don't like movie stars anymore
I love the stars I haven't seen
          one in months
I hate this city I love its blacks in their
clothes of flags and legs like streets
                          love Michigan Ave
where the godlike white building got completed while
      I wasn't looking no one possibly works in it
          hopefully
          monument-
al I'm so little it feels all right to be like a
      twinkle in a creek at night or the tiniest bell
              in the wind that empties me
              into the tiniest sound
                          equal to any
no believing
          nothing in blue nothing in black

FOR ALL THE SONGS I SING

for Petrarch

Do the largest stars terminate the world?
The mirror a great play picture a distorting ton pickup
Drastically reduced for immediate sail
    Holy air untroubled by the full of my desire
A great play novel motion
                I'm folded down
              like an angel's down
            a great gesture,
          to a fair bough
          the earth so gently
        a great gesture
              ever folding, turning

Linger and see my passionate peace of heart
Desire high
Above a calm sea of stars
Weaving from it a circlet for her
Blazing hair
Miracle to be crushed against such dreams
Boldly
Bodily
My strolling pensive wit
Perhaps composed in 1346

How often then I said
If thouds't more apparel and holy will
Thou coulds't have broke the spell but
    Beguiled I chanced to be
    My darling cheat
    Composed it would seem in 1345
Insatiable, which famous donation
   I suffer, byde I
      Fair stream, flowing past Vaucluse,
      In honor of Laura
    Perhaps for the anniversary of his enamorment

105

In that sweet smile is her
        lovely face
And in that

            That no mere star
                        Now deeply black

        Her usual elegance laid aside
        You'll stand dazzled weeping forever at
        The mind's clear record
                        I left
    My heart
                With her
                        An instant only

TRIBUTE

Here's a quiet tributary
stream to the Snake:
the bees keep the pollen and
the honey going around.
Once in a while a moose
meets a bee. Wow. Now
there's a hurt moose.
Moose kiss makes it well.
Trumpeter swans are like
the eagle, beautiful
and faithful. The ghost
of the unquiet father waits
patiently in the brush
hundreds of hours to get
the picture you seem.
And so I am mean.   Flowers

cradle, thorn, bird, this
world, composed is a
surface one's tension will

define. The amount of
the unknown rising in one's
time in the universal soul.
Waking ideation, down
by river, can't see

Boundary Cone; dreaming the
French notice some piece
of the chair they're
interested in, say 2 legs,
then, photograph it. I
think I draw it all I
don't know how to draw.
And then I do. It
protests very subtly from the
spring of government,
drawing delightful to
the floaters. Their

color is gold and they
thicken it, for the winter
months ahead. A Fall
is a time to re-
member. Something about the
sunlight flashing on their
loves, and when you love
a wilderness you know some
things will never change.
My moose kiss goes
on forever.

IN THE ART INSTITUTE LIBRARY...

The nun bent shameless
        snoring—
the Venus turned out to be exquisitely
        small—has from under black

"attached" kind earlobes and golden
           glasses
the lamp shade most beautiful is green lit
                                    oh
the stairs were sagging but the
           high lights are
globes
           and you walk up them
and are startled by a beautiful
           black man
                      he doesn't
take you in hand
                      and your
card you're a member
turquoise and golden red, for example
"he would go out saying something
           about Kiss-
then return to the game"
                                on masks
                                          our faces naked
with a beautiful secluded
garden "What do plants live on?
                                mystery"
strips a wine-colored cape
a pride of hearts sky himself
love sublimated
                "good grief"
oh. The snores of a nun
                                are holy
in that they force
                      they grant
the lady behind her
                      annoyance change smile
                                          her own
benignity
           we see a sweet and funny that
membership that rises up
                                around her
the exact likeness
                of days that go by
impressed her lips on a fresh collar
as traditionally American as
I think probably the best human
           cry in paint

Mike Tappin

DARLENE PEARLSTEIN

Darlene Pearlstein was born in Chicago in 1952. She received a B.A. with a teaching certificate in elementary education from The University of Illinois at Chicago Circle. A founding editor of The Milk Quarterly and a director of The Yellow Press readings at The Body Politic. *Rabbits, Frogs and Other Mischief*, her book of children's poems, is in a second edition. Her poems have appeared in Child Life, Telephone, Matchbook, Community of Friends, and The Milk Quarterly. Anthologized in *Jukebox Poems* and *The Alphabet Anthology*. Currently a full-time teacher in the Chicago Public Schools.

4/20/75

Tired of this urbanity
we're off at last
for points unknown
can't wait to see
my first truck stop
passing through
toll gates will be
thrilling as will
pay toilets
Ah, but
mountains of
mountains are
waiting
They've been hanging
around for centuries
just for me
primping themselves
to perfection
knowing that
soon they will
migrate
and become
islands
in the sky

4/22/75

Wonderful day
Wonderful country
Eyes opened
to beautiful
new sights
as we speed

along vacant highways
through Tennessee

No noise
just music
Birds and lizards
whisk through leaves
Minding their business
as we mind theirs

Trails to climb
Staircases of
roots and branches
Cascades and
Waterfalls
rush down
to meet us
and the river below

Country kitchen
Sweet smells
of mountain air
and wild flowers
make me hungry
and want to stay

But we rush on
to meet the Smokies
but find them
in shadows
as the stars
freckle the evening sky

5/2/75

Been working
on that old

Guttenberg line
Printed matter
doesn't matter
My hands are
tattooed with
postmarks
but there are
no stars
to illuminate
this inky
darkness

Predawn riddles
intrigue me
As do sunbeams
and starfish
I've been fishing
in muddy streams
No trout here
But I've got
a line on you
My minnows
imitate pearls
and send
the moon
rushing for
cloud blankets

5/5/75

Hold that
umbrella
high over
my head
I need
a little

protection
today
My raincoat
is too
loose
to provide
adequate shelter

Cold slips
into my
bones
like dimes
hiding in
the corners
of my pockets
The cloud bank
has gone out
of business
and the sun
is on vacation
as I turn
right past
the vernal
equinox

5/30/75

They've
given us
this day
to pull out
memories
like old
tissues
and blow
our noses

on them
again
This is
a recession
and everything
must be used
to capacity
Even the dead
must contribute
as an energy
source for
the living
Yeah,
there's
a skeleton
in my closet
and one
under my bed
You can smell
the decay
as the
visions linger
Just one more
for the road
Just one more
before I
ask for
the keys

6/10/75

I'm spooked
and swelled
with exhaustion
Need to have
this tank

drained and
unclogged
Air filters
through worn
perforations
Got to get off
this bed of nails
Will trade
or exchange
portfolios
for action

10/17/75

Sleep insures
an added identity
returning
undercover
with confidence
Roll me over
to Ontario
and back
again to Rome
I've got
some miles
to put on
this sea
of alpha waves
I'll get off
without a trace
I leave no
fingerprints
and polygraphs
catch themselves
in their own lies

Eyes in waking
position they
refuse to see
But give me
the shade of
evening and
blinks become
nods as I drift
on rubber thoughts
guaranteed to leak
and simmer me
in my own
renaissance

11/16/75

Eyes blink
in unequal
proportions
Each has
an offer
Drift off
to dreamland
or face the
bowl and examine
the ingredients
I postpone
the decision
forcing the
demons back
Punching bags
bags of paper
Each take
the shape of
their contents
as I slip
off the sleepwire
writing lists of
things to do

11/22/75

Just keep
inflating
and patching
up those
inner tubes
that give form
to our souls
Not an easy job
when perspective
is your only tool
and the electric bill
has not been paid
The circle is not
the ideal shape
My configuration
for contentment
has not yet been
defined and I'm
still walking on
the periphery
Toeing the perimeter
of that perfect polygon
the adrenalin flows
and offers the
only excitement allowed
But I insist on danger
I resist all impulses
to stand still
Let me provide
my own motion
I've got a
definite swagger
I've got my own
intervals to unveil
A sculptor neglecting
the footprints of
those who've tried
to move in
Arms full
slamming the door
with my foot

Dennis Bayzer

BARRY SCHECHTER

Barry Schechter was born in Chicago in 1948. Graduated from the University of Illinois at Chicago Circle. Credits include *The Iowa Review*, *Chicago Review* and *The Paris Review*. A book, *Come As You Are*, will be published by The Yellow Press.

ON MY 26TH BIRTHDAY

In the reference room a man is flipping pages.
To read faster, says Evelyn Wood
ignore words
concentrate on patterns, blocks of print
columns of words
marching double-time
to the bottom of the page.
Eyes turning like odometers—
10,000, 15,000 words per minute—
he wants to read *all* the books,
like a man walking faster and
faster through the Louvre
till his hunger for images
makes him race past flashes of
green wheat, tumbled fruit, and luminous flesh.
Today I'll read want-ads,
phone friends who aren't home,
and watch the monotonous rain
the way he flips, now, through a second book.
Unfocused,
his eyes are like the splotch of light
on the table's brown unpolished wood.
I dreamed once of drowning
and, instead of my life,
I saw patterns of words, blocks of print,
columns of dolls unfolding from shreds.

PRACTICING MY DEATH

On the beach among the sunbathers
I practice my death
My dark suit and tie
blot up the sun like thunderclouds
My pockets bloat like sandbags
In the dark above the sheets
my raw face burns like a shrine

I'm the man who
sits up on the coroner's slab
and says "Just testing."
You see, there's this mortician inside me,
correcting my postures,
adjusting my smile
to put you at ease.
When I lean
forward, like this, and my
smile reminds you of
porcelain set out for a special occasion,
it's all quite painless, and even pleasant.
I'd hate to embarrass you, in the end,
with an involuntary grimace.
I'll pose for death
ankles crossed, hand tucked
behind neck, like a boy dozing in a hammock.

On all the sidewalks
the same corpse keeps turning up.
Shopkeepers are closing their awnings.
But I only want to put you at ease.
I'm alive, you see:

That isn't sawdust

leaking from my hollow spaces,

it's only sand.

PROFILE

For years I was known as The Great Profile. I gave up the other half of my face as if it were an ugly Siamese twin. I was a poet, and poetry had turned my head. You see, I could never decide whether to write for everyone or for one reader: so I read poems to the empty space just above her left shoulder. People thought I was a visionary. I spent an entire year in three-quarter profile, staring past every shoulder. By now I was writing entirely for Posterity, which I conceived as the sum of all those empty spaces. I lived in a Phantom Zone where elbows poked me and voices swore, but I never saw a face. Audiences at poetry reading thought I was looking straight into heaven: I was staring into corners where mops leaned like the ragged survivors of a depopulated planet. Invisible coteries guided me through the streets.

Once I stared into a corner and saw an apparition beneath the fire-exit sign. It was my discarded quarter-profile, cold and dead as a meteorite. So much for Posterity! I gave my head an extra quarter-turn, and here was the profile of the poet laureate suitable for tracing straight onto a medallion. I didn't feel as if I'd torn myself in half, but as if I'd chopped away rock from the outline of a perfect sculpture. I strode sideways through adoring crowds, till the day my perfect profile crashed through a storefront. I was uncut, but so ashamed I wanted to turn my face completely, like the moon darkening into its final phase. Instead I began turning the other way, and with the humility of a pie-spattered comedian slowly revealing his features, I looked straight into your faces.

THE LITTLE HAT

For the sin of pride the authorities made me wear this little hat. It fits me no better than a baby turtle, this blue plastic derby secured by a rubberband round the chin. Though I was allowed to stay on in my high position, my authority was subverted like a poster scrawled over with mustaches and black teeth. The hat defaced my famous scowl, transfiguring it, in the eyes of subordinates, to the grimace of a rambunctious birthday-boy. Some men can meet the Queen with spaghetti in their hair; can cartwheel down the street in Bozo masks and command the dignity of a passing funeral. But I was never the naked emperor: I can make men stammer and stare at their shoes, so long as my tie-clip is in place. Conspicuous? I might as well have donned the Taj Mahal as that tiny plastic derby!

For a while I made *everyone* wear little hats. But they seemed oblivious to their duncecaps, fire hats, derbies and stovepipes: they didn't share my disgrace; they only mirrored it. One clerk, seized by the holiday mood, tooted a sneeze-horn in my face!

Once I tried concealing the problem beneath a full-sized bowler. But a cop snatched it off my head and the little hat shined like a naked turtle.

THE NATIONAL ANIMAL

When it was first placed in my care, it seemed forlorn as a dented hat. Years ago my parents had taken me to see this animal at Marshall Field's. It occupied the throne usually reserved for Santa. My father lifted me to its ear. The words didn't echo, as I'd hoped, but sank under drifts of white fur. Laughing, my father said that he, too, would speak to the National Animal. But he looked serious when he parted the fur and, leaning close, whispered. I could not find the animal's eyes but imagined they'd be like headlights seen from high in the air. Now, years later, here were the eyes: dried peas in a plate of leftovers. And here were these men from the government telling me I'd been selected as keeper of the National Animal.

Why did the dilapidated animal arouse not pity, but anger? When we took long walks the animal's fur, matted with spit and thrown stones, resembled a mop that cleaned out the filthiest recesses of hatred. My landlady put us both on the street. My employers told me the animal was strictly my problem goodbye. Like mongrels clutching the last shred of domestication, we clung to our identities as animal and trainer. I'd whistle the old patriotic tunes and the wheezing animal would leap through an inner tube. The trick it grew to like best was playing dead. One day I bent over the ratty fur and put my mouth to the ear. The words, as always, sank into silence. "Quit falling back on the easy stuff; let's try a triple-flip arabesque." But the animal of course was dead.

Suddenly the entire country is mourning. Children send me their pets, to console me for the National Animal. Sometimes they paste on cardboard fangs and antlers, for its image has already become hazy. One writer contends that the National Animal was never very important anyway. What was important were the words we whispered into its ear. Remember how the words seemed to drift under the fur? It will take a long time to bring them back.

NOT A CLOWN

First, I am *not* a clown. Clowns are paid to make you laugh. *I'm* paid to laugh. Listen. You see: the effect is like a firecracker in a barrel of mousetraps—if you're in the vicinity, laughter springs open your jaws. Commentators, attempting to explain this contagion, note that I never laugh the same way twice. My laughter must supply a hidden meaning of the joke, they say, like the exegesis of a text. But my mirth isn't confined to jokes. Does it point to inexpressible meanings in *things?* There is a guffaw, for example, for the tree near my window, that tattered old man insisting on the same monotonous gesture. There is a chortle which is the chord of three ideas struck at once: a man carrying a hatrack; a wishbone in the center of an enormous plate; an idiot watching a snowfall. The titter signifying death is so faint it touches the ear's canal like a reflected star. But what of the laughter that seems to come from nowhere? It is with this that I have had my great success in curing the insane. They tell me they had been reaching for this laugh in the first place, like a man who, groping for a lamp, thrusts his finger into an open socket.

THE WHY BOTHER CLUB

A sigh escapes—falls, really, like a corpse from a closet. A butler gathers the untouched drinks, the newspapers sliding from laps, the dangling phrases intoned from deep within the upholstery. "I'd like. . . . ." "You'd like what, Sir? Another paper? Another drink?"

Here is the Major. Remember the day he addressed your Scout troop? His white hair and beard were well-groomed as a crack team of sled dogs. His self-discipline seemed to extend even to his internal organs, bellowing "Single file!" to blood cells in the tiniest capillaries; or reprimanding the small intestine. "This is peristalsis! Not a goddamn discotheque!" But one day he began to relax. He fell off barstools casually as a Dip-the-Man. Knots of fat spread over his frame like bed-sheets flung over a prison wall. "I'd like. . . , " he says.

Here is the billionaire, whose only desire was to be surprised. His hit-men fired near-misses till the weave of trajectories grew homey as an old sweater. The schizophrenics he hired to crash his parties were predictable: when they wrote on the walls in excrement, he'd pick up a handful and complete the sentence. Last week an undaunted madman burst into the Club and posed a riddle to the billionaire: "Bathing stinks. You know why?" The billionaire answered wearily: "'Cause you're in the service. Can't quit when you feel like it." "I laid off cigarettes," said the madman, "because you're in a spatial condition," concluded the billionaire, "from outer space yourself, thirty-three years this June." Ignoring the maniac, he turned to the butler. "What I'd like is just a very *tiny* surprise. Probably something you could buy in a novelty shop, right next to the joy buzzers. I could buy out the whole line and check the inventory, but. . . .

"'. . . why bother,' Sir?"

"Of course."

And now the butler is approaching me. I order another drink, which I leave untouched beside me, and another newspaper, which I immediately drop onto a large pile. Crumpled drafts of "The Why Bother Club" are scattered over the floor like a conclave of senile brains. The butler gathers the crumpled sheets, my drink, the newspapers. I have sunk frighteningly deep into this chair. How long have I been here?

"I'd like. . . ," says the Major.

"A drink, Sir? A paper?"

Very quietly the Major begins to speak. "The skull of a camel is cool to the touch. You won't forget. It was Africa in '42. The Sherman Tank, goddamnit, was a percolator with men inside! Awful rough going in the desert. Where does the next breath come from? My pennon was a bright yellow with one blue chevron. You and your canteen and on the turret wall a calendar, that's right, held by a wire. Sandgrains stuck where you sweated. You can't help thinking about that when you look at your discharge papers. Sand everywhere. Froth? Caused by the sun? Well, the distinct impression that someone tampered with your life. Sometimes the treads of armor on the move snap like a ripcord. Must there be a reason? I heard a story about this dalmatian, friendly like, mascot for the whole neighborhood you could say. They find it one day minus a front paw, sawed clean off. The vet is called in, but a couple of weeks pass and a rear leg is chopped off. No one knows who. After a while all the dalmatian's limbs are missing, and some girl hears its howling until she catches sight of it by the light of a streetlamp. What looks like a spotted laundry sac spinning and crying. I put my feet into the Mediterranean. Calm for a body of water, like on the maps in the geography book as a kid. Weeks after I'd fascinate myself with the shine of a cigarette case. I held it at angles. This brought back to me how I wanted my life to be a point faroff in the water. I must have ordered my column to a halt. My pennon was a triangle beaten by the wind."

(with Peter Kostakis)

Other Yellow Press Books:

Red Wagon — Poems by Ted Berrigan

paperback ISBN 0-916328-01-5 $3.00
cloth   ISBN 0-916328-05-8 $7.95

Alice Ordered Me To Be Made — Poems 1975
                                      by Alice Notley

paperback ISNB 0-916328-02-3 $2.50
cloth   ISBN 0-916328-06-6 $6.95

Straight — Poems 1971-1975 by Richard Friedman

paperback ISBN 0-916328-00-7 $2.00

Yellow Press Books are distributed by Serendipity Books
1790 Shattuck Avenue, Berkeley, California 94709
Please Order from them

No variety about the moon. It comes and goes like
the milkman and the moon's milk is always the same.

—Raymond Chandler